David Anfam
is a critic, curator and a leading
authority on modern American art.
His books include *Franz Kline: Black & White,
1950–1961* (1994) and *Mark Rothko: The Works
on Canvas – Catalogue Raisonné* (1998), which
was awarded the 2000 Mitchell Prize
for the History of Art.

Thames & Hudson world of art

This famous series
provides the widest available
range of illustrated books on art in all its aspects.
If you would like to receive a complete list
of titles in print please write to:
THAMES & HUDSON
181A High Holborn, London WC1V 7QX
In the United States please write to:
THAMES & HUDSON INC.
500 Fifth Avenue, New York, New York 10110

Printed in Singapore

Nancy Tilden 05

Abstract Expressionism

David Anfam

169 illustrations, 28 in color

 Thames & Hudson world of art

ACKNOWLEDGMENTS

Because a book of modest length devoted to such a sprawling subject as Abstract Expressionism can hardly find the space for footnotes my primary debt is to the writers whose scholarship goes mostly unacknowledged in the text – the groundwork laid by William C. Seitz, Meyer Schapiro, Clement Greenberg, Irving Sandler, Dore Ashton, William Rubin and Lawrence Alloway, and others numerous enough to make a summary list impractical. If the present study, though often at variance with them, manages at least to balance personal views and historical facts upon their foundations it will have served a purpose. In a far more general sense the acumen of Frank Kermode's writings has been another stimulus. I should also like to mention the past guidance of John Golding at the Courtauld Institute. In America Kate Rothko (Prizel) went beyond all reasonable kindness and previous vicissitudes in giving access to a select record of largely unknown works by her father which demonstrated the significance of the movement's earliest stages. The library and staff of the Museum of Modern Art, New York, and the Archives of American Art were both of special help, as indeed were many American museums and private owners who enabled me to study their collections. I have benefited from discussions with Lynne Cooke of University College London about de Kooning's sources, from Aaron Siskind's efforts in tracing photographs and my publisher's patience. Mrs Clyfford Still's exceptional generosity in permitting the reproduction of certain works by her husband must also be recorded, as should the fact that their interpretation remains mine alone. Finally, this book could not have been completed without the encouragement and support of Fred Bearman and, not least, my family.

© 1990 Thames & Hudson Ltd, London

First published in 1990 in paperback in the United States of America by Thames & Hudson Inc., 500 Fifth Avenue, New York, New York 10110
thamesandhudsonusa.com

Reprinted, with revisions, 2002
Reprinted 2004

Library of Congress Catalog Card Number 89-50635

ISBN 0-500-20243-5

Printed and bound in Singapore by C.S. Graphics

Contents

CHAPTER ONE

Introduction

Abstract Expressionism is a landmark in the general history of art and of modern art in particular. Like the Cubist epoch it represents a revolutionary event which revises our view of things before and after. Only in this case even the modest historical distance separating us from those early years of the century is not yet available and what began with the rise of the movement shortly before the Second World War opens perspectives that enfold the present. In microcosm we might compare this to the far vaster shift which saw America itself command the centre of Western political power and culture after 1945. Together the two developments indeed thrust that country for the first time in history to the forefront of the visual arts, a sphere in which it had always traditionally either imitated Europe or followed its own eccentric patterns. Both changes took place with unusual speed and thoroughness, provoking many at times contradictory explanations, and are responsible for some of the more familiar cultural emblems of the sophisticated postwar West.

As Hollywood, Coke or a Ford soon became part of the everyday geography of experience, so the most famous instances of Abstract Expressionism have provided readymade symbols of modernity to our cosmopolitan eyes. Jackson Pollock's mazes of paintwork, Mark Rothko's hovering rectangles and Willem de Kooning's strident *Women* possess the same sort of currency as Mondrian's grids, Picasso's multi-faceted faces or Warhol's *Marilyns*. It was in Toledo, Spain (not Ohio), that I recently saw a car patterned with 'Pollock' splatters (similar jeans and T-shirts are indeed already left-overs from the 1970s) while Rothko could pin to the studio wall an urbane *New Yorker* magazine cartoon showing 'sunsets' imitating his icons well within his own lifetime. Yet for all its cachet Abstract Expressionism will probably never quite find the audience that embraces Impressionism nor the outright popularity enjoyed by Salvador Dali or David Hockney. For that it remains a shade too serious, strange and extreme, like Cubism itself.

1

6

13

2

7

1 Jackson Pollock, 1950, photographed by Hans Namuth

"Now, there's a nice contemporary sunset!"

Of course such superficial facts can be overstressed but they point to something altogether nearer the heart of this art: its capacity to be at once striking yet inwardly complex, to invite multiple interpretations alongside even the attacks and misreading which canonical works alone manage to survive. Canons in the arts, as the literary scholar Frank Kermode has observed, tend to be shaped by a curious mixture of opinion and knowledge, ignorant bias and informed intent. Their formative process is therefore rather interestingly broached through photographs and cartoons or other parodies which, in tending to record surfaces, also often exploit the deeper levels of our psychology and social experiences. Thus the couple bemused in front of the Rothkoesque sunset touch upon the artist's tantalizing combination of poetic colour and an apparent blankness supposed to show contemporary art's emptiness. Further myths together with some revealing truths are projected through the numerous photographs and portrayals of Pollock and his painting, as good an entry as any to the subject.

Efforts to stereotype Pollock and by extension the works of his colleagues started soon enough with photographs originally meant to

2 Rothko 'Sunset' cartoon, *New Yorker* 29 November 1964

3 Jackson Pollock, *Life* 1949, photographed by Arnold Newman

© Arnold Newman

accompany a 1949 *Life* magazine story. In conjunction with the 3 sceptical article published that year they pictured an aggressive brooding figure who would have been identified with the emergent wave of hooliganism in America then and whose creations epitomized the destructive, violent chaos of 'modern' art. At his death in 1956 *Time* ranked 'Jack the Dripper' beside the other now openly named 'Wild Ones' in a reactionary estimate that has endured under some remarkably changeable guises.

A few are forthright like the 1962 *Saturday Evening Post* cover by 4 Norman Rockwell which reduces Pollock's delicate lines to a wall of splashes that leaves the spectator cold. A more ambiguous romanticism has sensationalized the topic and especially Pollock (on whom several biographies have appeared to date) as the tormented artistic genius second only to Picasso, drowning his private demons beneath tangles of pigment. Less gross if equally naive was the account popularized by the American poet–critic Harold Rosenberg in a famous *Art News* article of 1952 wherein 'the canvas began to appear to one American painter after another as an arena in which to act –

9

4 Norman Rockwell *Abstract and Concrete (The Connoisseur), Saturday Evening Post* cover, 13 January 1962

rather than as a space in which to reproduce, re-design, analyze, or "express" an object, actual or imagined. What was to go on the canvas was not a picture but an event.' Without any nameable content Abstract Expressionism could be portrayed as new and unpremeditated. Rife during the 1950s, this myth faded once knowledge of the earlier work restored a perspective to the later and best-known phase, showing the content and forethought behind it. Disregard or hostility, however, continued with Tom Wolfe's 1975 satire *The Painted Word* which claimed that critics just injected

5 Jackson Pollock painting *No. 32* 1950, photographed by Rudolph Burckhardt

meanings into the images and, perhaps more unexpectedly, with recent Marxist historians who perceive 'decomposition', 'alienation' and 'negation'. All these models are inclined to mistake actual themes – dynamism, chaos, space, traces of the human presence – for somehow involuntary or detrimental eruptions. Plainly, Norman Rockwell's parody and Pollock's *Lavender Mist* (1950) attest to the difference.

4, 98

Pollock posed for a second category of photographs in 1950 which present a more positive image contrived to emphasize his tough, virile

5

gesturing at work and his cowboy persona at rest. That these call to mind other paeans to rugged American values such as the famous *Life* photograph by Joe Rosenthal of the imperious Marines, reconstructed (as was the painter) in their raising the US flag on Iwo Jima in 1945, offers evidence towards a longstanding identification of the whole movement with America's search for a national identity. 'Rawness', 'vigour', 'bigness' are time-honoured stereotypes to characterize the New World and these qualities have been held to stamp Abstract Expressionism as somehow reflecting a native character. According to Robert Rosenblum and others, the grandeur of the continent's landscape is resurrected in the immensities painted by Pollock, Rothko, Clyfford Still and Barnett Newman. Even in the first comprehensive and authoritative account in 1970 Irving Sandler was moved to celebrate 'The Triumph of American Painting', a title which supplies fair praise besides a distinct bias: how would it now sound for example if 'France' or 'Italy' were the victors?

Certainly several Abstract Expressionists advertised their American roots but as one facet out of many and no one-to-one parallel exists between their aesthetics and the country. This is where the two other main interpretative trends lack balance. Serge Guilbaut's polemical *How New York Stole the Idea of Modern Art* (1983) concentrated on the supposed lack of overt political statement in the paintings which allowed them to be exploited by dealers, galleries and writers as propagating freedom and individuality in the Cold War struggle against Communism. Consequently it illuminated more the background chicanery than the art. The reverse applied to Clement Greenberg's theory of Modernism (here capitalized to distinguish it from its broader historico-cultural sense) as a progressive effort to purify the properties of a particular artistic medium. In painting these amount to colour, surface and the delimitation of flatness so that when Abstract Expressionism exploited them (for indeed it did) this revived, according to Greenberg, a tradition last kept alive by Cubism and created in the words of his eponymous 1955 essay an '"American-Type" Painting' hoisted aloft over European beginnings.

Our problem now seems less that these various accounts ring true or false than that they remain too exclusive for art and artists who above all strove to be all-inclusive. Few artistic phenomena this century push us further towards Coleridge's quixotic wish for 'one central perspective point' where all the fragments of truth will knit together. Few also elude it so consistently. But unless we attend to the centre the margins are bound to dominate and Pollock saw himself most definitively amongst over five hundred photographs – the number itself telling a story – that he allowed Hans Namuth to take during the summer of 1950. These offer another myth (and one distorted by Rosenberg) except that it fulfilled Pollock's own wishes by enriching, not narrowing, interpretation. Under Namuth's lens he dissolves into spangles of light, hurtling after-images and the patterns of flung liquid while still present as the source, or even a part, of the energy. Turning to the paintings done that year, like *Lavender Mist*, we find a parallel richness able to absorb all the opinions about flatness, violence, the luminous grandeur of space and so forth without being exhausted. Ultimately their subject rests upon their extraordinary structuring and Henry James would have identified it when he wrote: 'Experience is never limited, and it is never complete; it is an immense sensibility, a kind of huge spiderweb of the finest silken threads suspended in the chamber of consciousness, and catching every airborne particle in its tissue.'

1

98

Reviewing Pollock's open-ended status and accomplishment prepares us for the 'set of shifting positions about an unknown center' by which William C. Seitz, author of the first proper history, *Abstract Expressionist Painting in America*, adroitly labelled his subject in 1955. Since then, no matter from what angle it has been approached, attempts to presume and write about a monolithic movement have failed because, quite simply, no such unity ever existed. Therefore the most that can be done is to recognize this heterogeneous make-up and aim at a compromise which captures its profile without destroying its variety. The time has also come to recuperate the early and late work, neglected altogether until the end of the 1970s, and restore them to a whole.

In the case of the actual name, 'Abstract Expressionism' constitutes another unwanted title alongside 'Fauvism' and 'Cubism' which was chosen, though not invented, by a *New Yorker* critic rather than any insider. Rival terms still current include Rosenberg's 'action painting', which possibly owed not a little to the notion of wartime 'action' photography, and the more respected 'New York School' designation. But the first at best covers just Pollock, de Kooning and Franz Kline, whereas the second has no descriptive value whatsoever, misleadingly implies some chauvinistic band of successors to the School of Paris and is a misnomer in relation to Still, who lived a mere twelve out of his seventy-six years in the city, or to David Smith and Pollock, whose most productive times were spent upstate in the Adirondacks and out near the easternmost tip of Long Island.

'Abstract Expressionism' at least has the merit of denoting extremes, the breadth that extends from Newman's abstract and measured chromatic panoramas to de Kooning's fierce expressionist figuration. Nonetheless, it fails to indicate how even those boundaries have fluctuated.

The photograph entitled 'The Irascibles', taken by Nina Leen of *Life* magazine for its 15 January 1951 issue (since reproduced often enough to have become a cliché), was long considered to show the Abstract Expressionist pantheon gathered to protest against the conservative anti-modern exhibition policies of the Metropolitan Museum of Art. Instead it was more a hurried assembly of figures who had no common manifesto other than their 'irascible' opposition to an outside enemy. Unlike most previous avant-gardes they remained too individualistic to accept a group identity. 'With us,' said Newman in 1965, 'only the individual artist can die or continue to grow and live.' Yet there is still scope for a more representative selection than the fifteen individuals rounded up by *Life* and it is only fair to note that both Jimmy Ernst and the single token woman, Hedda Sterne, were there more or less by chance and find no place in the present study. On the other hand, the choice of those included calls for justification.

Although Pollock, de Kooning, Still, Rothko, Newman, Kline, Philip Guston, Arshile Gorky, Robert Motherwell and Adolph Gottlieb are by consensus prime members of the Abstract Expression-ist canon, it has not always been so and the exact repute of each continues to be debated. Until the 1960s Newman was marginalized and Guston considered a secondary figure, while of late Pollock's pre-eminence has been questioned. As already suggested, such ebb and flow belongs to canonical formation itself and this book adds its own emphases without pretending to be a final or, in view of its length, exhaustive account. The first six painters cited above receive somewhat more attention because in the key period up to the early 1950s one or another made unique or notably original statements. So did Gorky at the last despite his untimely suicide, whereas Kline matured in 1949–50 by developing what others had already discov-ered. Of Gottlieb and Motherwell it would be fairer to say the opposite insofar as neither went on to consummate their innovative wartime works with the masterpieces that otherwise sealed the end of the decade, notwithstanding the second's splendid eventual resur-gence. Bradley Walker Tomlin, Theodoros Stamos, Richard Pousette-Dart and James Brooks fall, I believe, into a second rank – latter-day Marcoussis and Metzingers, piquant yet peripheral. Nor were Hans Hofmann and Ad Reinhardt central on this reckoning. Hofmann's expertise in pictorial mechanics learnt firsthand amongst the European avant-garde made him the technical tutor to Abstract Expressionism but otherwise he skirted its symbolic, existential foundations. Reinhardt declared himself an outsider socially as well as aesthetically and often satirized his sometime colleagues. His faith in geometric design went against their principles yet an emotive streak belied that apartness and at the last suffused his finest paintings. Hence his career traces, mostly from without, a kind of boundary line.

Prejudice alone kept Lee Krasner outside standard histories: the telephone call she answered asking her husband to join the 'Irascibles' extended no second invitation. In fact, her fellow artists held the same assumptions about gender that most Americans had then. At one of their hangouts, the Cedar Tavern, Krasner recalled women being 'treated like cattle' and, conversely, dominating feminine imagery is a sub-theme in de Kooning, Smith, early Still, Rothko and Pollock. Those seem good hunting grounds for Freudians and feminists; suffice it to say that the woman tagged 'Pollock's girl' deserves a place, late developer as she was, in any balanced survey. Ideology also structured the narrow framework which excluded sculptors and photographers since they remained during the 1940s and after the poorest of relations to American painters in the marketplace, critical forums and paradigms of the 'fine' arts. However, Smith maintained 'I belong with painters' and few American photographers have so deftly penetrated that difficult zone where they infringe upon painting as Aaron Siskind. The last point perhaps renders him more 'Abstract Expressionist' than other contenders such as Minor White whose cosmological mysticism rather than epic boldness belongs with Mark Tobey's to the West Coast. Furthermore, Siskind and Smith underwent almost identical formative influences and expressed the deepest themes that – reluctant as one is to define a crux – preoccupied their fellow painters and around which Abstract Expressionism turns in all its diversity.

'We are concerned with similar states of consciousness and relationship to the world . . . If previous abstractions paralleled the scientific and objective preoccupations of our times, ours are finding a pictorial equivalent for man's new knowledge and consciousness of his more complex inner self', wrote Rothko in an exceptionally straightforward statement published in the 8 July 1945 issue of *The New York Times* and from first to last Abstract Expressionism is saturated with references to the human or animate presence.

Once noticed, the theme becomes visible everywhere. By default, Hofmann considered nature 'the source of all inspiration' while Reinhardt preferred a pure non-objectivism. Leaving them aside, this concern hallmarks the origins of the movement in works dominated by the figure and its surrogates, or else pulsing with bodily rhythms, and then, once an abstract zenith had passed by the early to mid 1950s, it motivated neo-figurative tendencies. Smith's numerous vertical (sometimes outspread) protagonists illustrate another version and so does Siskind's quest for organic, physiognomic or 'active' forms against their opposites such as gloom and flatness. It precipitated the portrayal of fragmentation, death, rebirth and symmetry (all corporeal states) during the 1940s together with a primitivism that stripped humanity to essences, to *Male and Female* (c. 1942) as one Pollock title proposed. Abstract Expressionist space is also often irreducible to figure and ground, as with the superimposed layers in Rothko's *White Band* (1954), *Lavender Mist*'s explosive spray and Smith's decentralized constructions. We distance the world by drawing boundaries between the self and space and these works undo it, merging solid and void, questioning where we end and they begin. At its keenest the stress on apperception gravitates over to us – the creative audience who must decode de Kooning's *Excavation* (1950), read substance where Smith supplies contour alone in *Hudson River Landscape* (1951) and become the third force meeting the other two, one perceptually very near, the second distant, that emblaze the darkling blue of Newman's *Cathedra* (1951). As Smith wrote in 1953, 'a work of art or an object is always completed by the viewer.'

Consciousness as a leitmotif evolved from the acute self-awareness of the artists themselves. Time, identity and their relationship to the world were fundamentals. Several appear to have been jolted into pondering human destiny by personal circumstances. Gorky and de Kooning knew the immigrant experience, Still battled with the anachronistic plight of a homestead on the Canadian prairies after the First World War and Rothko, born into a poor Russian Jewish family, faced WASP anti-semitism at Yale in 1921–23 and saw himself as an outsider to a hostile society. Guston too hailed from the Jewish slums of Montreal and after the family went to Los Angeles in 1919 his impoverished father committed suicide. Fifth son to ne'er-do-well farmers, Pollock suffered from deep insecurity, failed to stay more than a year in successive high schools and tended to alcoholism even as a teenager. This, then, was the last artistic generation to internalize romantic stereotypes (Guston kept a print of Dürer's *Melancholia* on

130

63

6

86

101
124

120

16

6 Mark Rothko *White Band (No. 27)* 1954

the kitchen wall) which heavy drinking, defiantly intransigent behaviour (Still, Smith) violent deaths (Pollock, Gorky, Smith) and general bohemianism hardened further.

The personal stances would make mere biographical melodrama had they not conditioned the art. Smith's sculptural ambition – to be technically brilliant (he lectured on chemical formulae and analysed paints), abstract, didactic and concrete – was amplified via such declared roles as industrial labourer, backwoods hunter, Schoenberg aficionado and an essayist who announced in a 1959 speech, 'this work is my identity'. Newman consented to pose before his canvases. 7

7 Barnett Newman, 1963, in front of *Onement VI*, photographed by Alexander Liberman

8 Jackson Pollock *Self-Portrait c.* 1930–33

9 Arshile Gorky *Self-Portrait at the Age of Nine, c. 1913 c.* 1927

10 Clyfford Still *Self-Portrait* 1940

12 Mark Rothko *Self-Portrait* 1936

11 Franz Kline *Red Clown* 1944

Thus their grandeur mirrors an august self. Rothko once considered becoming an actor and in a prescient 1936 canvas fills the frame yet chooses to reveal little in retreating behind darkened lenses. All stricken ego, Pollock instead stares wide-eyed from a grainy vignette of obvious Romantic pedigree while Still's strikingly assured 1940 *Self-Portrait* suggests someone already aware of his place in history who remains nonetheless singular. The many personae of Gorky are perhaps the most calculated. His *Self-Portrait at the Age of Nine* (c. 1927), for example, bestows the style and even physiognomy of Cézanne's *Louis Guillaume* (c. 1882) upon an imaginary ego. It is as if artistic practice were being plotted through the various selves.

A heightened sense of time stimulated a need to master it that is evident in Still's 1935 graduate essay on Cézanne, Smith's 'I suppose historians will be able to find reasons to suit their needs why we have happened' (1955) or when de Kooning interjected at a symposium, 'it is disastrous to name ourselves' (1951), as though they might thus escape history's filing cabinet. Here Nietzsche was influential, anticipating a distrust of language responsible for pronouncements often couched in metaphor, poetic diction or shorn phrases. Still's elimination of titles, followed by Rothko and Pollock in the later 1940s, had similar causes.

But in one primary matter they were all the century's children: a generation that came to maturity in the wake of a world war, followed by the Depression, the Spanish Civil War, global conflict again, Holocaust and nuclear apocalypse. By Newman's reckoning they knew 'the terror to expect. Hiroshima showed it to us. The terror has indeed become as real as life' (1945). A traumatic zeitgeist is discerned easily enough in Abstract Expressionism's daemonic figures and fractured forms, the sombre ritualistic atmosphere, unsparing surfaces, exacerbated drawing and a more brutal aesthetic norm than the spiritual and sometimes utopian abstraction of predecessors like Mondrian, Malevich or even Kandinsky. These constitute what Gottlieb named in 1947 'the expression of the neurosis which is our reality'. Another side to this eschatology was the rejuvenation that burgeoned soon afterwards. Colour and light flood several artists' images, Smith's sculpture gains a heroic or soaring appearance, de Kooning's *Woman I* (1950–52) is resurrected, sky re-enters Siskind's frame, Kline went from introversion (*Red Clown*, 1944, is a melancholic alter ego) to his extrovert maturity and Pollock achieved for his painting a vibrancy foretold by Newman's in the essay quoted above: 'Let us, rather, like the Greek writers, tear the tragedy to

13 Willem de Kooning *Woman I* 1950–52

shreds.' The modern human predicament therefore appears broadly etched in this *agon* or journey between dark endings and dynamic beginnings.

Despite the 'big' existential signposts ('tragedy, ecstasy, doom', said Rothko) that echo previous responses to cultural despair like German Expressionism we are still faced with the most difficult, because layered, art since Cubism. Originating when it did – around 1930 onwards – the backcloth of modernism (including Greenberg's specific formalist definition already cited) lay ready for the taking. Even its boldest effects cover this intricacy which Motherwell caught when he said, 'every intelligent modern painter carries the whole culture of modern painting in his head' (1951), and Reinhardt could

14 draw a cartoon by 1946 whose tree of modernism has his colleagues amongst its leaves. Nietzsche, Freud, Jung, Whitman, Joyce, Eliot, Einstein, myth, primitivism, Neo-Platonic leanings, the stream of consciousness, Mallarmé's pregnant void, the relocating of the beholder . . . the list of sources either overt or tangential feeding into the movement is a modern genealogy. Cubism itself, Surrealism, Fauvism and expressionist traits (particularly as filtered through Beckmann, Orozco and Siqueiros) provided the givens of its formal syntax; Krasner's career, for instance, ran its course between Picasso's drawing and Matisse's colour. The fact that axioms of painting, sculpture and photography such as their respective flatness, mono-lithic nature and innate naturalism are rethought and dramatized here also attests to a radical modernist quest for new languages.

Whether indeed feelings and ideas can somehow be embodied in what we see raises an old philosophical quandary that the artists themselves mostly bypassed since they assumed the drift of Eliot's famous 'objective correlative' (it had numerous descendants in the intellectual air of 1940s America, as discussed in Chapter Four) whereby an image need not describe but would, like some essence, encapsulate a whole emotional complex. Rothko remarked in 1959 that 'a painting is not a picture *of* an experience, it *is* an experience' and along similar lines Motherwell believed that 'the "pure" red of which certain abstractionists speak does not exist . . . Any red is rooted in blood, glass, wine, hunters' caps and a thousand other concrete phenomena' (1944). The special regard for *techne*, materials, physicality, therefore deserves mention. The phenomenal liquidness

98 of *Lavender Mist* seems to reify a split second for ever, a veracity about Siskind's focus suggests (to borrow Gottlieb's memorable phrase) 'the

127 beginning of seeing' and Rothko after 1949 saturated his thin glazes

14 Ad Reinhardt *How to Look at Modern Art in America, P.M.* 2 June 1946

with dry pigment so that the crystals suspended in their microstructure reflect back light to create an inner glow. Further instances of this technical striving, such as the widespread use of enamels and impasto or Smith's experiments with polychrome and the welding torch, are already presenting ominous problems to conservators, but they give a generous and quite unmistakable physical force to Abstract Expressionism at its best.

CHAPTER TWO

Background and Early Work

America emerged from the First World War as the world's leading creditor nation and the next decade witnessed such economic growth and optimism that many believed a capitalist utopia had finally arisen. In 1919 Congress rejected Woodrow Wilson's efforts to secure the country's participation in the League of Nations and the following year Warren Harding was elected on a pledge to 'think of America first'. His successor, Calvin Coolidge, summarized the prevalent ethos: 'the business of the American people is business'. Prosperity during the 1920s was grounded on huge industrial expansion and resulted in an aggressively 'modern' era of consumerism, mass culture and technology. The increasing affluence, ease and – to some thinkers – senselessness of American life since 1945 is the message of the 1920s writ large.

Behind these changes stood the moving force of the machine. Between 1917 and 1929 new manufacturing processes and numerous accompanying mass production techniques burgeoned. Cars, film, radio and the telephone transformed communications and ultimately human relations, making the tenor of existence faster, more impersonal and even inhuman. By 1920 over half of America was judged to live in cities, once places of fear and loathing but now seen as loci of excitement and power. Since these new features looked at once interesting and strange, American culture became a focal topic. Writers such as Waldo Frank, Lewis Mumford and William Carlos Williams studied the national heritage, while the visual arts returned to homegrown subjects. These had never been altogether discarded anyway insofar as the 1913 Armory Show, the first real platform for European modernist painting and sculpture, made a relatively transient impact upon an ingrained realist predisposition, an empirical eye, stretching back to Eakins in the nineteenth century and renovated by the Ashcan school painters shortly before and during the First World War. Unlike earlier self-examinations which looked to Europe for their benchmark, this laid bare two distinct mentalities.

15 Charles Sheeler *Upper Deck* 1929

Ideas of order dominated one standpoint, reflecting a brave new world where the machine, the city and objects themselves were paramount. Williams's poetry encapsulated this attitude and settled on concrete images and detail, true to his slogan, 'no ideas but in things'. The real subject of John Dos Passos's key novel *Manhattan Transfer* (1925) is New York, the Jazz Age metropolis rendered as a collage of facts which reduces the human element to a mere agent in an empire of force. In painting Charles Sheeler had already treated such indigenous themes as Shaker architecture as early as 1917, employing clear geometric planes influenced by Cubism yet without its fragmenting lens. Over the next decade this immaculately sharp approach spread (including photography as well) and earnt the generic title of Precisionism. Nature rarely disrupts its often man-made but cold environment. Like most of Sheeler's works, *Upper Deck* (1929) is depopulated and its complex of svelte metallic elements evokes the certitudes of impersonality. Thus far Precisionism was in step with much European art of the 1920s which presupposed few questions about the individual. For just as the 'moderne' style of the time was meant to bring a clean, well-lit future to the present, so the large streamlined form would become a symbol of public confidence during America's Depression, whether in the sweep of locomotives, buildings or idealized landscapes.

15

But the beginnings of Abstract Expressionism took shape against both this optimism and another more negative vein which the Depression would intensify. Although America championed material progress it remained a wasteland to those who preferred human and spiritual values. For expatriates like Ezra Pound it was ever 'a half-savage country, out of date' and Sinclair Lewis in *Babbit* (1922) satirized an emotionally barren American stereotype eventually known to the 1950s as 'the Organization Man'. Such disaffection was to be repeated by Clyfford Still, David Smith and others who noted America's sterility and alienation, a theme already current in literature from Eugene O'Neill's dramas to the novels of Hemingway and Scott Fitzgerald. In particular, William Faulkner's remarkable phase of literary experiment initiated by *The Sound and The Fury* in 1929 had a sombre inward tone which paralleled that of the Abstract Expressionists in combining realism with a symbolic or experimentally subjective intent.

Before the Depression few artists had fathomed this second more negative seam but amongst the exceptions were Charles Burchfield and Edward Hopper. In motifs like the deserted buildings painted in the early 1930s by Pollock and Still echoes of Burchfield occur, just as the isolated figures in Rothko's pictures from then show Hopper's influence. Crucially, the third factor which moulded this younger generation was the Depression itself. Insofar as the economic collapse after the 1929 Crash seemed to undermine the era's dynamism it reinforced an older popularist belief that has surfaced cyclically in crises, according to which the nation's true voice is supposed to sound from its grass roots level. Against the facts of industrial decay and the big city with its foreign influx, artists and writers reacted with other myths as when Paul Rosenfeld wrote in *Port of New York* (1924) that after Europe had fallen into disorder due to the war 'we were thrown back on ourselves to find inside ourselves sustaining faith.' In painting Thomas Hart Benton and Grant Wood developed Regionalism and were joined by Southern Agrarian writers who reasserted traditionalist styles and ideas through versions of the American scene fabricated from rural nostalgia. Hence the Depression initially saw images or myths of the city and the heartland confront those from the 1920s in a social framework more marked than before by leftist beliefs, anxiety and divisions.

These contradictions reverberate in Pollock's early work for he actually studied with Benton and absorbed his teachings yet went his own way. He was born on 28 January 1912 in Cody, Wyoming.

16
17

18, 19

16 *top left* Charles Burchfield *Black Houses* 1936

17 *left* Edward Hopper *Sunday* 1926

18 *top* Grant Wood *Spring Turning* 1936

19 *above* Thomas Hart Benton *City Activities – Dance Hall* 1930

Of poor Scots–Irish ancestry, Pollock was shunted at least eight times in the next twelve years through the unromantic farming backwaters of California and Arizona. The family at last settled near Los Angeles where Pollock briefly attended high schools and formed a friendship with Guston before leaving to enrol under Benton at the Art Students' League in New York in 1930. Exposed to a declining agricultural way of life, with a redoubtable mother and rather depressive father, he seems to have had the aggressiveness that comes from pure insecurity, a fear of many things. Pollock's remove from the outside world
8 emerges in the darkly neurotic first *Self-Portrait* (*c*. 1930–33) which supports his claim in 1929 that 'people have always frightened and bored me consequently I have been within my own shell . . .' An aversion to conventional religion, shared by the other Abstract Expressionists, hid a search for wholeness. At an early stage ideas from such fashionable sources in California then as theosophy and Krishnamurti guided him towards a lifelong pantheism. Unrest at the flux of existence was to be countered by an urge to encompass it. Thereafter Pollock's art repeatedly confronted disintegration, entropy or violent motion.

Landscapes and figure pieces done before about 1938 show Pollock, who was clearly always ill at ease with the third dimension, transforming Benton's scenarios. Crude surfaces together with a vigorous attack repeat his mentor's notion that such traits revealed
23 directness and authenticity. But *Camp with Oil Rig* (*c*. 1930–33) and *Going West* (*c*. 1934–38) are already far from prototypes like Benton's *Boomtown* of 1928 and his other scenes of confident westward journeying. Life and colour are instead drained from the former with its props scattered over a desolate earth whose curvature becomes a tumult of all nature in *Going West*. Elsewhere throughout the early works this swirling upheaval draws the human presence or its surrogates into some greater overall rhythm.

That initial gloom is normally attributed to Pollock's admiration for the melancholy nineteenth-century American romantic Albert Pinkham Ryder, and the turbulence likewise attests to his studies after Mannerist and Baroque masters including El Greco and Rubens.
20 However, *Going West* further suggests an awareness of Turner's
21 *Hannibal Crossing the Alps* (1812) with its similarly prominent orb in

20 Jackson Pollock *Going West c.* 1934–38

21 J. M. W. Turner *Hannibal Crossing the Alps* 1812

the sky, driven figures, rocks and in particular a wrenching vortex-like organization. In the vortex Pollock probably saw a symbolic configuration keyed to his concern with polarities because its shape imposes wholeness upon chaotic energy, pulling outer limits towards an inward focus. Variations of its thrust pervaded his subsequent motifs (one painting from around 1947 was even entitled *Vortex*) and already in *The Flame* (*c.* 1934–38) hints of some violently figurative subject contend against the sheer rhythms of brushwork. Indeed Benton had argued that the figure and design in general were reducible to angular schema but what is prophetic in *The Flame* is the lozenge pattern within its welter of strokes – similar to the oval vortex of *Going West* – that prevents complete disarray. The momentum of applying paint has therefore itself begun to convey both chaos and ordering. If an apprenticeship in Regionalism taught Pollock to deal with personal experience, within only a few years he had otherwise left its commonplaces behind.

22

So too did Clyfford Still whose origins compare with Pollock's. Again, his family were of Scots–Irish provenance and moved soon after his birth on 30 November 1904 in Grandin, North Dakota, to Washington state and thence kept a homestead on the Alberta prairies. There his experiences proved decisive. The struggle to farm in a

22 Jackson Pollock *The Flame c.* 1934–38

23 Jackson Pollock *Camp with Oil Rig c.* 1930–33

basically hostile environment swiftly worsened after a series of droughts began in 1917. Later the Depression turned an already collapsed economy into a wilderness again and even the landscape seemed to reiterate this hostility since the vast flat horizons reduced any human presence to a mere vertical accent. That the region aroused complex and even contradictory emotions in the artist was evidenced when he went back to it in 1946 and referred to a 'lostland'.

Although predominantly self-taught, Still at least registered at the Art Students' League for the 1928–29 session (while Benton was there) and his early prairie scenes accord at face value with the Regionalist stress on the local habitat as a suitable starting point. These notwithstanding, *Row of Grain Elevators* (1928) and the rather later 26 (1936) scene of houses at an Indian reservation in the Washington 24 mountains run at a tangent to Regionalism, a hallmark of early Abstract Expressionism which is clearest in its distance from the popular optimism and even utopian side of the New Deal era.

24 Clyfford Still *Houses at Nespelem* 1936

Whether by Still, Pollock, Kline or de Kooning (who painted a brooding nocturnal *Farmhouse* in 1932), these are less tributes to nature outright than dark pastorals mindful of the human condition.

With its lateral elements correlated around a central massive focus, *Row of Grain Elevators* replies to Benton's precepts about pictorial balance expounded in an article of 1926. This seemingly academic search for a symmetry of sorts, where the bright red of a railway carriage at left counterbalances a green placed on the far side, would recur transformed in Still's most abstract works and so did the palette-knife technique. Here it is deft; twenty years on the results were to be surfaces scathed with violence. Nor could the sordid mechanical debris of the foreground have come from Benton or Wood with their buoyant folksiness, and his contemporaries from the 1930s recall the artist's moralizing eye even then. Before an expanse of sky the grain elevators rise above this disarray. Uprights that oppose their flattened surroundings occur in other compositions of this period and grew from a conviction that the space of the prairies had to be challenged by the 'vertical necessity of life'. In the study of buildings at the Nespelem reservation done in the year after Still wrote a trenchant analysis of

Cézanne the desolate note is stronger, akin in mood to Burchfield, whose empty houses are a haunted version of Regionalism, and to Pollock's treatment of a comparable abandoned factory at this time. Barren hills spread behind the architecture to repeat that symbolism of polarities – vertical against mass, presence in front of surroundings – which embodied Still's true subject from the first. 16

Around 1934 Still turned aside from moralized landscapes to concentrate upon the human figure. Compared to all the contemporary realisms the protagonists in these early paintings evoke the sheer plight of existence with an expressionist rawness. Distorted, journeying through darkened landscapes or isolated in space, they imply a *mythos*. By around 1936 he portrayed a male–female pair, a 25 union in partition, interlocked within a dry grey field that brings the picture-within-a-picture of Picasso's allegorical *La Vie* (1903–04) to mind. Lithe yet bulging limbs – which had been Benton's stock signs for human vitality – now become labyrinthine conours while the despairing gestures and blind looks find their counterpart in the rasp of the palette knife's scrapings. Already, much of the future Still is here.

25 Clyfford Still *Untitled ('Two Figures')* c. 1935–36

26 Clyfford Still
*Row of Grain
Elevators* 1928

It is in the unique and almost 'Nordic' vision which combines forcefulness and austerity, an attention to the picture's margin (the woman's hair is bright yellow) and the acerbic tones heightened, at the nipples, by crimson accents.

Franz Kline represented the third Abstract Expressionist from a relatively rural background, the coal mining region of eastern Pennsylvania around his birthplace of Wilkes-Barre. To allocate each artist to town or country makes less sense than to observe how some wished their roots to be thought integral with their artistic make-up. So Pollock and Still emphasized their Western beginnings, Gorky his Armenian background and Smith an early contact with steel working. Kline's renderings of Pennsylvania and New York obviously enough foretell the abstractions after 1950 in their blockish and dynamic structuring. They also possess idiosyncrasies standing in much the same relation to the future as the skewed *Red Clown* did to his own better-known exterior as the onetime high-school star athlete and All-American wit. Often there are pictorial obstacles, dark entrances or dishevelled arrangements which, like his introversion, were mostly but not entirely sloughed off in the otherwise imperious manner that eventually gained the upper hand.

As a youth studying art at Boston University (1931–35), in England (1937–38) and then resident in New York, Kline admired Rembrandt, Goya, Manet, Sargent and Whistler, all masters who had telescoped painterliness and drawing. These conventional sources, rather than the more sophisticated theories soon to develop in New York, convinced him that brushwork was indicative of a painter's energy. Here it is also noteworthy that he evinced considerable interest in the cartoon, a medium whose conventions for representing action are of course linear schema. Somewhat oppressive interiors and portraits from the early 1940s reveal that an academic training also taught Kline to compose in simplified masses with an angular armature underneath. *Palmerton, Pa.* (1941) portrayed his native locale from memory (like almost all the landscapes) as if no longer present to experience but still vivid in the mind. Together with other vistas, notably the fifteen-foot long mural of *Lehighton* (1946, commissioned by the local American Legion Post), these project what might be called a ramshackle panache which invokes the spirit of the place even as their locomotive power, literal and visual, runs aground on niggling detail and oddly foreclosed compositions. It is this unstable relation of part to whole that anticipates the zigzags lurching beyond the edges of Kline's later canvases while they still mesh internally into barriers or blockades.

27 Franz Kline *Palmerton, Pa.* 1941

Despite David Smith's ultimate pre-eminence as a sculptor, painting was his first pursuit and the great scope of his output came from straddling the two media. His investigations of different techniques and ways to redefine the three-dimensional object were invested with an imaginativeness that appears in essence pictorial rather than gravity-bound. To sculpture he brought more than someone born straight into the discipline might have done and thus his work belongs to Abstract Expressionism from the start in its medley of realism and psychologically charged expression, which centred upon violence, energy or other disturbing themes from the 1930s onwards. Smith and the painters alike then progressed to more abstract languages that retained a meaningful impact. At their root lay a shared involvement with the human presence or its substitutes and the forces threatening its integrity.

39

Decatur, Indiana, where Smith was born in 1906 and then the Ohio of his formative years epitomized the small-town culture which (like Still, Pollock and Kline) he saw permanently altered by a growing technology. By 1925 Ford made a Model T every ten seconds and when Smith went to work that year as a welder and riveter for Studebaker it brought him into contact with what he would henceforth regard as the century's dominant force: the machine and its embodiment in the industrial materials of iron and steel. By itself this was nothing new, since the 1920s, from Le Corbusier to Precisionism, had been a romance with industrial utopias. Yet Smith jettisoned that straightforward optimism and identified mechanistic power as double-edged, a threat to humanity and an instrument of its deep-seated urges. Two statements from the early 1950s summarized this symbolic understanding of his favoured materials: 'Possibly steel is so beautiful because of all the movement associated with it, its strength and functions . . . Yet it is also brutal: the rapist, the murderer and death-dealing giants are also its offspring.' And, 'The material called iron or steel I hold in high respect. What it can do in arriving at a form economically, no other material can do . . . What associations it possesses are those of this century: power, structure, movement, progress, suspension, destruction, brutality.'

Having gone to New York in 1926, Smith studied at the Art Students' League under the Czech Jan Matulka who encouraged the distinct textural contrasts in his first curvilinear Cubist paintings which grew from collages into low reliefs and then free-standing objects. Smith observed, 'Gradually, the canvas became the base and the painting was a sculpture.' After assimilating a pot-pourri of influences including the most recent European art movements (mainly via magazines) and African sculpture, Smith's education in modernism continued at firsthand during a trip to Europe in 1935 that took in Moscow, Paris and London. In any case, his mind moved quickly between disparate contexts and the sculpture would always juggle far-flung references with fixed themes that surfaced once he set up a studio in 1933, by a characteristic choice, at the Terminal Iron Works factory in Brooklyn. *Saw Head* (1933) adopts the technique of welding together ready-made metal parts that he had met on the production line and which so impressed him in the sculptures of Picasso and Julio González. By any standards this sympathy with constructivist principles was far-sighted given the traditional backwardness of American sculptors, ever stuck between the grand and the trivial, who by then were belatedly responding to an avant-garde taste

28

28 David Smith *Saw Head* 1933

for direct carving as practised by William Zorach and John Flannagan. Unlike the assemblages by Picasso and González from around 1926 onwards, *Saw Head* seems less concerned with poetically 'discovering' a countenance in found objects and more an ambiguous mask of power, cruel in its serrated edges yet vulnerable owing to an almost Cyclopean eye, paint that resembles rust and the ultimate lack of a solid core.

At the end of the decade Smith made a clear personal statement in fifteen *Medals for Dishonor* (*c.* 1936–40) influenced by Greek coins as well as German medals and Sumerian seals seen at the British Museum. All the obsessions that were to be transmuted in a further quarter century's sculpture are present in these nightmarish, strongly left-wing tableaux whose graphic character announces Smith's faith in drawing as communication, a probe that he said was 'closest to the true self'. The gross draughtsmanship of the *Medals*, emulating intaglio and Picasso's broadside-cum-comic strip *Dream and Lie of*

29 David Smith *Medal for Dishonor No. 9: Bombing Civilian Populations* 1939

Franco (1937), constitutes rough material awaiting refinement. In
29 *Bombing Civilian Populations* (1939) a sentinel statue is torn open to
reveal gestation within while leaden missiles replace or penetrate life.
Vital and morbid forces, metal versus organic suppleness are already
the latent issues and were to become the poles of Smith's work,
generating its dialogue between open forms and enclosure, thrust
against curve. The *Medals* confirm their source in a world where
humanity was threatened, partly by its own technological prowess.

Whether overt or subdued to unease, a similar response to the 1930s
informed the work of Guston, Rothko, de Kooning and Siskind. As
immigrants or the sons of such families they showed little obvious
attachment to place or native landscape. Rather, the urban dimension
can be sensed behind the tense alienated atmosphere wherein people
and surroundings sometimes barely cohere and it was Rothko who

spoke for them all when he looked back on this period and lamented that 'it was with the utmost reluctance that I found the figure could not serve my purposes . . . But a time came when none of us could use the figure without mutilating it' (1958). Eliot's 'unreal city' and 'hollow men' are not far away.

Philip Guston's first paintings located the disquiet in a political sphere. Coming from a family that had fled the Tzarist pogroms and soon drawn to socialism like his fellow Jews Rothko and Siskind, Guston knew about oppression at large as well as the more local activities of the Ku Klux Klan (whose membership reached five million in the 1920s) and other traumas in the Los Angeles of his youth, the flagrantly corrupt WASP-controlled metropolis that is the setting of Raymond Chandler's novels. The hooded armed protagonists in Guston's *The Conspirators* (1932) and his 1934 mural for the 30 palace of the former emperor of Mexico, Maximilian, refer to kindred menaces. All the same, these paintings aspire to a breadth founded upon Italian Renaissance art, Picasso's ample Neo-classical manner and de Chirico's stark perspectives. Content and handling therefore coexist with some irony since the average Social Realist would have pinpointed a more topical message and indeed the pencil study for *The Conspirators* showed a lynched black high up in the background. Instead, illustration is annulled as slyly as his hankering after a Grand Manner. We confront a figure scene without faces, drama without action and, as the hollow foreground element implies, volumes that are mere shells. Even the situation belongs as much to the props of the Hollywood studio – Guston then sometimes acted as a film extra – as to Quattrocento settings. This is the first of his many compositions where the covering, the residues of a known reality, are uppermost.

American culture between the Wars vibrates with society's noise and movement: in the crowded novels of Dos Passos, James Farrell and Thomas Wolfe, American Scene painting and its cast of picturesque 'types', and the advent of the sound film itself. Dissent from this norm implied a gulf between the private and social realm and though relatively rare included such important artistic documents as Hemingway's earlier writings, *Call It Sleep* (1934) by Henry Roth, Hopper's paintings and Walker Evans's *American Photographs* (1938). Each deployed either silence, inaction or the isolated individual – elements shared with the early work of Guston, Siskind, de Kooning and Rothko who echoed their introversion. Each also put an ostensible realism to unusual ends. One might go further still and remark upon a constant that almost defines the origins of Abstract Expressionism. It

amounts to a puzzling quality of narrative suppressed or made secret. What we see is sufficiently occult to indicate a larger life outside the frame, of events and climaxes either just past or about to happen. Pollock's *Going West* conveys this as surely as de Kooning's transfixed sitters. So does the lighting that is crepuscular in Pollock, frozen in de Kooning and Rothko's subway series, or encapsulated in Still's Nespelem scene by what he said of Cézanne: 'the light suggests no particular time of day or night; it is not appropriated from morning or afternoon, sunlight or shadow.' Rather than lay all these features at the doorstep of *pittura metafisica* they are better considered as rudimentary signals of an involvement with time and its arrest.

Around 1932 Siskind (himself a native of New York's Lower East Side) began to photograph its poorer quarters, adhering to the kind of documentary approach upheld by the Film and Photo League, a typical artists' group of the Depression with Communist links and of which he became a member. Yet strange accents intruded. Light and shade, detail or flat signs vie with people, a shrouded statue looms 34 ominously and an immobile figure is contrasted against a wall that is blank except for enigmatic graffiti. That the city had its less familiar aspects was already well known. In 1915 Paul Strand had photo- graphed New York with its populace dwarfed beneath huge vacant 33 expanses and to the Marxist Mike Gold in his ghetto novel *Jews Without Money* (1930) it is 'all geometry angles and stone', a view reiterated by the 1930s photographs of Rudolph Burckhardt, a close and influential friend of de Kooning's, which accentuate flat architectural surfaces. This was also the ambience which played an important part in Rothko's contemporary paintings and came to a climax in his scenes of the New York subway. 31

Misleading comparisons between Rothko's most famous icons and the luminous images of nineteenth-century Romantic landscapes lead one to expect that the scenery of Oregon where his family settled must somehow have impressed him profoundly. It did not and he even flatly denied this long after. His late 1920s watercolours of the Portland region are technically accomplished extensions of John Marin's crystalline idiom but hardly anything more. Instead his ongoing need seems to have been to deal with the human drama. How else are we to explain an initial *faux-naif* painterliness that owes not a little to the art of the children whom he taught at the Brooklyn Center Academy and the unwilling, dreamy 'realism' – for quotation marks are unavoidable – of the ensuing 1930s phase except as essays in picturing inward states of mind?

45

30 Philip Guston *Conspirators* 1932

31 Mark Rothko *Subway Scene* 1938

32 Mark Rothko *Interior* 1936

33 Paul Strand *Wall Street, New York, 1915*

34 Aaron Siskind *Dead End: The Bowery* 1937

35 Willem de Kooning *Man*
c. 1939

36 Walker Evans *Subway Portrait*
1938–41

At face value Rothko's themes – women, urban scenes and interiors – sprang from the repertoire of his teacher, the pioneer modernist Max Weber, and accord with the quieter American Scene idiom of contemporaries like Isabel Bishop and the Soyer brothers. Yet within the naturalistic framework the figures subtly conflict with their settings. Symmetrical doorways, for instance, frame two nudes, others are caught in the corners of rooms and though a street will plunge into depth human beings remain apart in the foreground. *Interior* (1932) is reduced to a facade enclosing a group of women who are themselves recessed into an indeterminate zone. Paradoxically, the handling soon tends towards delicacy as if Rothko had learnt from his early involvement with watercolour to layer the application of paint in variously scumbled and scratched passages. To search for an exactly defined 'subject' is to miss the whole point since the early Rothko is consciously reticent, just as his future art would be hard to summarize even as it prompted interpretation. Already flatness counters depth: facades after all announce what is behind them yet hide it. And if Hopper surely prefigured these juxtapositions of sensuous figures and sparse architecture, Walker Evans's photographs prove anyway that the notion of life ceding to the inanimate was a leitmotif of the Depression.

42

48

The series of portraits de Kooning did towards the end of the 1930s (besides his far more abstract compositions) cast a similar doubt over what they seek to portray. He had left Holland in 1926 and the legacy of a training in draughtsmanship at the Rotterdam Academy of Fine Arts survives in their precisely delineated faces and anatomy only to yield in turn to numb expanses bereft of finish or focus. To earn a living de Kooning painted features on mannequins during these years and his figures always retained a resemblance to the wide-eyed stare of dolls. *Man* (*c.* 1939) shares in a predicament that came to the fore 35 during the Depression and was exemplified in novels such as Faulkner's *Light In August* (1932) and Richard Wright's *Native Son* (1940) whose main characters lack identity, cornered between definition and a void. Also close to de Kooning's idiom (apart from its references to Mannerist portraits, Ingres and Gorky) are Walker Evans's New York subway photographs of 1938–41 (and again 36 Burckhardt did similar studies) which portray urban inertia through the gaze of those caught unawares, at once passive and unquiet.

When Rothko himself depicted the subway after 1936 the results were meta-landscapes of the city's nether regions, not wholly new as Reginald Marsh and Joseph Solman (with Rothko a member of the splinter group called The Ten) had already treated it, preceded by

Orozco in a sharply constructed series of 1928–29 and Hart Crane who included an infernal underground sequence in his epic poem *The Bridge* (1930). Anyone who has travelled the New York system, however, will recognize the idiosyncrasy in Rothko's renditions. Claustrophobia is intimated by an imagery of descent and enclosure with columns that almost swallow the elongated figures and flatness becoming the real *dramatis persona*. Yet the subway's deafening noise is replaced by silence and Rothko probably remembered this when a decade later he mentioned a '*tableau vivant* of human incommunicability'. Furthermore, an emphasis on surfaces implies that much remains beneath the surface, especially since an erstwhile public realm has been turned into an existential space. How this could accommodate the lessons of modernist art from beyond America's shores was the wider issue that others faced next.

CHAPTER THREE

The Question of a Heritage

In April 1950 a three-day conference was held at Studio 35 on New York's Eighth Street where the sometimes contradictory discussion included exchanges about how the participants broke with tradition. De Kooning dissembled by invoking the cliché that Americans were less freighted with the cultural baggage that made French painting so refined while Gottlieb disagreed saying, 'if we depart from tradition, it is out of knowledge, not innocence'. These and further controversies stemmed from what Hofmann called 'the question of a heritage', a continuing debate about the priorities of the artist in America that had begun in the intellectual ferment of the 1930s. Prevented by the Depression and then war from making the customary pilgrimage abroad, a majority of the Abstract Expressionists were led to examine with exceptional rigour what Europe had to offer them. Upon being asked in 1944 whether there could be a purely American art Pollock replied: 'The idea of an isolated American painting, so popular in this country during the thirties, seems absurd . . .'

What constituted 'advanced' painting, sculpture and photography? Should it be abstract or representational? Would foreign influences vitiate or strengthen it? How ought one to reconcile the expression of feelings with the reality of the medium and that of the everyday world? Such questions surfaced in earnest during the 1930s and still reverberated through the Studio 35 sessions despite the inevitable silencing of their political aspects in the climate of 1950.

The problems of powerful content restricted by the realism associated with 1930s mural painting are illustrated by Guston's *Bombardment* (1937–38). Although this is Guston's *Guernica* in miniature he did not actually see the Picasso until 1939 and it shares the dryness and sharp perspective of many murals done for the Federal Art Project (FAP, see below, which employed Guston) and which now look dated by their attempt to model 'plastically' upon a flat surface as if Cubism had never existed. Indeed the extreme states rendered in *Bombardment* or Smith's *Medals* were associated from the Renaissance onwards with illusionistic modelling and deep spaces that would

37

37 Philip Guston *Bombardment* 1937–38

38   involve the viewer. Looking ahead momentarily to *If This Be Not I* (1945) helps to illuminate Guston's route past these dilemmas. Although still heir to the intricate battle scenes of Piero della Francesca and Uccello, this composition is also subtly conditioned by de Chirico again, Beckmann and Picasso's *Three Musicians* (1921). Unlike *Bombardment* it no longer forces realism: a more planar space mindful of late Cubism and Beckmann's compressed designs accommodates volumes and chiaroscuro. What was demonstrative before is refined into an issue of style. Instead of an image exploding from its confines, we are drawn inwards to fathom ambiguities.

    Although Guston's move to Iowa City to teach in 1941 anomalously placed him beyond the influences of the New York art world, *Bombardment* shows what he left behind in its affinities with the Social Realism favoured under the FAP. The FAP was part of the Works Progress Administration (WPA), a part of Roosevelt's New Deal

38 Philip Guston *If This Be Not I* 1945

relief schemes from 1933 onwards, which by its end in 1943 had included thousands of artists amongst its $8\frac{1}{2}$ million employees. Almost every major Abstract Expressionist already active in the 1930s (except Still who stayed in Washington state) worked for it at some point. Doubtless the 'Project', as it was then known, provided vital support to them in difficult Depression circumstances but whether it nurtured the formation of a New York avant-garde seems dubious.

Despite the roster of styles allowed on the Project, figuration was officially preferred and the distaste facing important public statements that opted for abstraction, such as Gorky's *Aviation* murals at Newark airport, had an alienating effect. In short one can imagine a stage in the later 1930s when most contemporary realisms – conservatively populist like Benton's or left-wing and humanitarian like Ben Shahn's – looked outworn to those who felt that Americans, as Pollock added in his 1944 interview, 'had generally missed the point of modern painting from beginning to end'. Perhaps the Project aided a sense of community but further factors hastened their notion of being an embattled minority waging war against provincialism, none less than their distance from Paris. It gave them the advantages reserved for *arrivistes*, what Lawrence Gowing has elsewhere called 'recruits in the hour of victory', and they were thus able to rifle this century's art movements with the licence that those nearer the scene of events never 42 had. Picasso was the exception and works of the type of his 1927 *Seated Woman* where Cubism, Surrealism and an expressionist urgency all blend held a special sway over them by the late 1930s.

New York City itself had changed a lot since Alfred Stieglitz's 'Little Galleries' (1905–17, afterwards '291') was a lone outlet for Marsden Hartley, Alfred Maurer and other first-wave abstractionists with whom, incidentally, the Abstract Expressionists had next to no contact. Now it provided a bird's-eye view upon modern art and its sources. This took in the A. E. Gallatin Museum of Living Art's important selection of French paintings, the Museum of Non-Objective Art (later the Guggenheim) and its numerous Kandinskys, forward-looking dealers like Julien Levy, J. B. Neumann and Pierre Matisse and, supremely, the Museum of Modern Art (MoMA) whose exhibitions (besides the ever-growing Permanent Collection itself) from 'Cubism and Abstract Art' (1936) onwards reviewed the pageant and background of modernist painting and sculpture. MoMA also amplified the theories of its curator Alfred Barr whose accompanying catalogues emphasized the self-enclosed vision of the innovative creator progressively disregarding society, he implied, to explore either abstraction or the unconscious. MoMA and Barr affirmed an emergent thesis in some New York circles that political engagement was not directly translatable into art, which obeyed its own laws. Simply put, social and aesthetic freedoms stood apart. Variations on this premise were legion. An untheorized instance was Gorky's remark that Social Realism was 'poor art for poor people', whereas the writers associated with the magazine *Partisan Review*, founded in 1934 on Stalinist lines, modulated by the close of the decade towards theories owing much to Trotsky's views about 'revolutionary freedom'. Amongst them was the young Clement Greenberg who edited the magazine from 1941 to 1943, befriended several Abstract Expressionists and would represent them as the vanguard of a new American art.

Trotsky opined that 'revolutionary' culture need not just mirror society but could leap ahead along its own trail of innovation and experiment. Like many Trotskyists, Greenberg's heterodox Marxism crumbled in the late 1930s as the Nazi–Soviet Non-Aggression pact followed revelations about Stalin's Russia. He then supposed the artists had followed his reaction against leftism by the 1940s, saying later that 'some day it will have to be told how "anti-Stalinism", which started out more or less as "Trotskyism", turned into art for art's sake, and thereby cleared the way, heroically, for what was to come.' That summarized Greenberg's private odyssey. Yet as a reading of Abstract Expressionism it rings false. Equally slanted are subsequent revisionist critics who portray it as 'de-Marxified' and then co-opted by postwar American conservatism.

Few Abstract Expressionists began as doctrinaire radicals and those nearest to that description like Smith and Reinhardt did not abandon their socialist principles afterwards. Newman remained a lifelong anarchist, Still intensely anti-authoritarian, and Pollock, so far as is known, kept his youthful leftist views. None ever believed in 'art for art's sake'. What did burgeon during the late 1930s was a conviction that meaning could be conveyed through the physical primacy of the medium. Here Greenberg was responsible for disseminating ideas and enthusiasms around a small artistic community centred on Eighth Street in Greenwich Village. Its nucleus numbered most importantly Hofmann, de Kooning, Gorky, John Graham, Lee Krasner and Greenberg himself. The first four were of foreign extraction (and the Bavarian-born Hofmann was thirty-two years older than Pollock), sensitized to recent European painting and consciously outsiders in a time and place where such influences were often rejected. Lee Krasner, who matured rather gradually into a strong painter, first met Pollock briefly at a 1936 loft party and they married in 1945. She was crucial in bridging his potential waywardness. Each of these figures either represented a wellspring of European discoveries or gave them another, inward tone.

Hofmann acted in the former capacity as a teacher, having founded his New York art school in 1933, who had known at first hand such eminences as Picasso, Matisse and Braque before he fled the Nazis. His classes are hard to reconstruct in detail, especially given his problematic use of English, but he must have widened the horizons of students and friends, arguing the need to synthesize Fauvism, Cubism and German Expressionism. Saturated colours, dynamic space and slashing brushwork in *Table with Teakettle, Green Vase, Red Flowers* (1936) 39 derive respectively from those movements. As the blue rectangle at the right arrests the red cabinet's plunge into depth it demonstrates his concept of painting as a self-contained equilibrium of advancing and recessive forces which he termed a 'push-and-pull' aesthetic. Thus Hofmann encouraged younger painters to understand the intrinsic potentials of their discipline and grasp how colour might create space more tangibly than illusionistic drawing alone. If before they had expressed psychological effects and states by exaggerating movement, stillness and so forth, Hofmann's instruction provided the rule that corrected emotion. 'Tension' here meant brushstroke and hue pitted against the resistance of the flat canvas. This reaffirmed a fundamental avant-garde tenet since at least Cézanne in painting and Stieglitz's pioneer efforts in photography: that to find equivalents for three dimensions within the pictorial limits of two was in itself a drama.

Notwithstanding, Hofmann had a more conventional outlook than most concerning nature. He saw it as a starting-point whereas they were subjectively inclined. As Pollock retorted to him at their first meeting in 1942 when rebuked about not working from nature: 'I *am* nature.' It may even have been this very lack of inwardness which, as György Lukács remarked in *The Theory of the Novel*, leads to a provocative instability between the world's space and the self, that explains the consistently more 'composed' look of Hofmann's work and its brightness in every sense. Krasner's charcoal studies from the life done in his classes strike out afresh even as they are indebted to her teacher's theory of empathy (oddly similar to Benton's premises) for their rhythmic clashing planes. Gritty and muscular, they bristle with Krasner's particular temper, not Hofmann's elegance.

By contrast John Graham proved to be more the theoretician and personal mentor, 'discovering' or encouraging Gorky, de Kooning and Pollock. Once a counter-revolutionary in Russia (yet quick to claim the artist for 'an enemy of bourgeois society'), a collector of African sculpture and knowledgeable about new Parisian events, Graham's intellect ranged easily from brilliance to absurdity and back, finding unexpected links between aesthetics, psychology and history ad infinitum. On the evidence of his book *System and Dialectics of Art*, read by the cognoscenti at its appearance in 1937, Graham embodied a fascinating storehouse of ideas and pursuits for anyone eager to escape provincialism. None would have meant more than his theory that abstraction distilled the essence of reality – unless it was the observation that a brushstroke constituted a record of personal emotion.

Gorky was the seismograph of these currents because he regarded the painting act as a means to establish identity. After a narrow escape

39 Hans Hofmann *Table With Teakettle, Green Vase, Red Flowers* 1936

from the Turks' genocidal campaign in his native Armenia he reached America in 1920 at the age of sixteen with a reluctant emigrant's typical obsession for the heritage of the exotic, partly medieval country left behind. His remark that 'an Armenian in America is a strange thing indeed' tells of dislocation and the literature is full of Gorky's calculated ethnicity, weaving legends and poetry around his origins so that his name (he was born Vosdanik Adoian) blended an Armenian royal title (the Caucasian 'Arshak') with that of Maxim Gorky. Insecure and suspended between a lost past and an alien present, Gorky's avid passion for art met an existential need. To become a great artist once he settled in New York in 1924 would validate his inheritance of Europe's cultural riches.

So thoroughly was Gorky immersed in the narrative which he felt bound to extend – nothing less than that of modern art itself – that over the next ten years or so he eschewed all conventional lipservice to originality. His techniques appear crafted in the same sense as when an artisan empathizes with a chosen master. Hence he claimed, 'I was *with* Cézanne for a long time, and now naturally I am *with* Picasso.' Adding a close analysis of Matisse, Braque, Ernst and finally Miró in the late 1930s, Gorky came abreast of European innovations ahead of almost everyone else and with quite different idioms at his service. Yet his own voice emerged. He was particularly attracted by the later so-called 'Synthetic' phase of Cubism typified by Picasso where, as in the 1927 *Seated Woman*, flat forms interlock in an ultra-shallow space. In *Organization* (1933–36) this vocabulary starts to feed into a personal

42
41

40 Lee Krasner *Nude Study from Life* 1940

41 Arshile Gorky *Organization* 1933–36

42 Pablo Picasso *Seated Woman* 1927

43 Arshile Gorky *Night-time, Enigma and Nostalgia c.* 1930–32

language. From an interpretation of Picasso's 1927–28 'artist and model' images it next passed through a more geometric grid-like state advised by Mondrian until, beneath thicknesses of paint, the subject disappeared into ciphers. The central black motif, for example, conjures both a palette and an organic presence with an inscribed cavity, breast or eye. Multiple readings were an old Cubist standby, except that Gorky found for them a space which would intensify metamorphosis and he lifted it, precociously, from Surrealism.

43   *Night-time, Enigma and Nostalgia* (*c.* 1930–32), predominantly a graphic series, represented a springboard for Gorky and was to generate pictures almost a decade hence. Several Surrealist sources coalesce here: abrupt perspectives from de Chirico and Dali, sculpturesque forms out of Moore or Arp which, in turn, dissolve to linear arabesques anticipated by Ernst's *One Night of Love* (1927). Darkness unifies them in a manner that his oils would not match before the early 1940s bringing erotic overtones that Gorky associated with nostalgia for Armenia. In writings his homeland was pictured in fertility symbols as a nature where matter moved easily, he stated in 1938, 'from one state into another.' So the sexual contours and spatial

44 Arshile Gorky *The Artist and his Mother c.* 1926–34

intricacy may be read as Gorky's processing of European borrowings through his private, folkloric imagination. To unite both he first had to recover the more distant heritage.

Numerous portraits of himself, family and even imaginary companions culminated in Gorky's two versions of *The Artist and his Mother* which occupied ten, perhaps fifteen, years of effort from about 1926 on. One immediate source was a 1912 photograph taken in

44

Armenia; further allusions are woven into the pictorial fabric, especially of the more resolved Whitney version, to Picasso's Iberian phase, Uccello, Ingres, Miró and Egyptian funerary portraits. But despite, or even somehow through its eclecticism, *The Artist and his Mother* is not quite like anything done before in Europe or America. Innermost memories are there, for his mother had died of starvation and a gap absent from the photograph now separates the pair. An opalescent light seals in any volumes upon themselves. The mother's face, a virtual death mask in the Washington version but constantly scraped or sandpapered down and repainted to glassy perfection in the Whitney's, is remote compared to those unfinished tactile areas where the pigment drifts loose. At one level *The Artist and his Mother* tackles ethnicity in the wake of the biased 1924 Immigration Act, the 1921 Sacco and Vanzetti trial (which led to the wrongful execution of these two immigrants) and widespread racial prejudice. At another it marks alongside the contemporary novels of Thomas Wolfe and James Agee's semi-documentary *Let Us Now Praise Famous Men* (1941) a disquisition upon time, self and experience. And the painting itself is visibly frozen overall in a process of change.

Through a close friendship with de Kooning, Gorky transmitted this idea of art as self-discovery. Why else did the younger immigrant, a stowaway from Rotterdam at the age of twenty-one, himself entertain a dialogue with the perceived signposts of the modern tradition (Cézanne, Cubism and Surrealism) and likewise refuse to settle for either the abstract or the fully decipherable image? It was an expressive conflict repeated by Pollock, Still and others.

A paradox attends any illusionistic effort to render substance and space on a flat surface and one has only to consider an almost legendary instance, the near-meeting of the fingers of Michelangelo's God and Adam on the Sistine ceiling, to understand how edges, points and emptiness carry a large burden of meaning in the process. In de Kooning's figure pieces after *Man* those efforts became obsessive. Some of his favourite exemplars like Ingres, Boccioni and Picasso's 'Analytical' Cubism had anticipated this, but hardly its magnification into a compendium of anxieties. *Glazier* (*c.* 1940) was described by de Kooning as 'the result of hundreds of studies on how to paint a
45   shoulder' and *Seated Figure (Classic Male)* (1939) is invaded by a flatness that pulls painting and drawing apart. De Kooning's friend the dance critic Edwin Denby was in fact then deconstructing the human anatomy with comparable ruthlessness in his essays and reviews. Lines and brushwork in search of a figure also furnished the basis for more

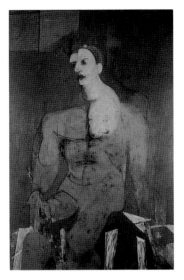

45 Willem de Kooning *Seated Figure (Classic Male)* 1939

46 Willem de Kooning *Elegy c.* 1939

hermetic compositions like *Elegy* (*c.* 1939) whose fleshy fragments are   46
squeezed into curt shuffling planes by the format, henceforth
seemingly a trifle too small for whatever de Kooning placed within.
Exposed underpainting heightens the effect by denoting a surface
resistant to closure.

The changes that de Kooning explored during these years
conformed to larger issues throughout the movement. Firstly, the
figure was replaced by cryptic surrogates, organic or quasi-geometric,
mostly imported from Surrealism or like tendencies and continuing
well into the 1940s. Secondly, more sophisticated spatial structures
emerged, in alignment with the picture plane or actually exploiting its
pressures. Behind each was the awareness that powerful content had to
be expressed rather than illustrated. In a 1937 review of Rothko's
group The Ten, the artist–writer Jacob Kainen, for instance, mentioned 'a complete and utter dependence on pigment as an expressive
agency rather than an imitative or descriptive one.'

The re-orientation of Siskind's photography in 1939–40 implies
that this assumption cut across a broad spectrum. From the former
year his close-ups of vernacular architecture in Bucks County,

48 Aaron Siskind *Chilmark 1940*

Philadelphia, isolate inanimate details and bestow a charisma usually reserved for the figure. Siskind said that music fostered his sense of the abstract and poetry his passion for conciseness. Space is foreclosed much as de Kooning had treated it, but there was also ready precedent in the work of the f.64 Group that included Edward Weston, Ansel Adams and Dorothea Lange. During the 1930s they fined down the photograph to a basically flat but brilliantly detailed record of things in their most essential form. But theirs was a classic purist vision which Siskind had the courage to deny when he went to Martha's Vineyard in 1940 and searched out 'the drama of objects'. Before walls, ground or other re-creations of flatness, fragments such as a fish-head, glove or the tines of a fork are stripped of their everyday veneers and become metaphors of death, sex and estrangement. Again, Surrealism and its bizarre Freudian objects are a precedent; again the consequence is just beyond that outlook with fantasy giving way to starkness.   48

Photography had an innate advantage at this stage since by employing factual elements it sidestepped the need to invent them

65

47 Robert Motherwell *The Little Spanish Prison* 1941–44

49 Mark Rothko *Untitled* 1939–40

afresh in a fabricated space. That became Rothko's task once he sought
to translate the mood of the Subway series into more universal terms
that would measure up to the scale of the troubled history of the West
in the late 1930s. Figurative remnants are located beside motifs meant
to evoke ancient and pre-human times and hence the whole cycle of
being. Roman or Etruscan sarcophagi and the Metropolitan's
72 Mesopotamian sculpture inspired *The Syrian Bull* (1943) and the tier-
like compositions he evolved beforehand which enclose heads, other
body parts and detailing. One thinks of the earlier measured
31, 32 architectural settings having intruded upon the figures, but Rothko's
antipathy to Cubism for a while left him without a usable past and
49 *Untitled* is too conceptual, a bare diagram of entrapment or of
consciousness divided into evolutionary stages. Revealingly, Robert
Motherwell's overview of art history, engendered by studies at
Harvard and Columbia, made his first endeavours from around 1941 a
response to this impasse. From John Dewey's philosophy he had learnt
to regard abstract rhythms as an expression of the inner self.

66

The Little Spanish Prison belongs to a 1941–44 sequence that   47
included *Mexican Night* and *Spanish Prison Window*. Together they
addressed what Motherwell thought was the decisive tragedy of the
era, Spain's Civil War, a symbol of the death of freedom. Wavering
bands of yellow ochre and chalky white inspired by the folk objects of
Mexico, a death-obsessed culture that fascinated the artist, prohibit
entry into *The Little Spanish Prison*. As a facade broken only by a small
magenta strip resembling a blank aperture it foretells the various grids
and labyrinths that became prominent in Abstract Expressionism in
the War years and connotated psychic frustration or deadlock.
Mondrian and Ernst had prefigured these designs yet not their
psychological overtones. Moreover, Motherwell's teacher at Columbia, the art historian Meyer Schapiro, would have alerted him to a
logic that justified setting European vanguard styles into a new,
symbolic and relatively angst-ridden context. As outlined in his 1937
essay 'The Nature of Abstract Art', Schapiro's intelligent Trotskyist
reasoning maintained that all culture was rooted in the social matrix,
hence there was 'no "pure art", unconditioned by experience'.
Nevertheless the status of abstraction remained unclear. Did it, in
other words, express alienation or freedom from life's tensions? Those
who championed 'hard-edged' geometric idioms and formed the
American Abstract Artists (AAA) in 1936 chose the latter conclusion.
    Reinhardt, another graduate of Schapiro's, joined the AAA in 1937
after studies under Carl Holty who had absorbed ideas from
Mondrian in Paris in the early 1930s. His cool, dispassionate early   50
canvases – in an internationally established Cubist–Constructivist
mode – acquire another aspect when judged as statements from an
even more socially aware sensibility than Motherwell's. Leftist beliefs
ought to have obliged him to dismiss non-objective geometry as an
ivory tower. Instead he saw its purity as a double-edged weapon and
in a 1942/43 discussion of Mondrian asked rhetorically, 'What greater
challenge today . . . to disorder and insensitivity; what greater
propaganda for integration, than this emotionally intense, dramatic
division of space?' Here he was trying to save abstraction from its own
sterility as if it might transcend chaos and the banal, rather as Wallace
Stevens had already said in his famous poem 'The Idea of Order at Key
West' (1935). Pictorially, however, this would always place Reinhardt
in a love–hate relation to Abstract Expressionism. Critical of its
romanticism, he shared its eye for absolutes.
    Before the Second World War Pollock, Smith and Still effected the
most complex reckonings with non-American sources. Without

Reinhardt's faith in geometric order they felt freer to experiment. In retrospect it seems hard to envisage where their respective *Going West*, *Saw Head*, or *Untitled ('Two Figures')* could progress without lapsing into story-telling or at least a too demonstrative art. That fierce expressionism called for another outlet and there was a restlessness about their search through Cubism, Surrealism and primitive influences as if they were quite certain of what to say but determined to shape it in a truly 'advanced' syntax. By merging such erstwhile separate idioms, like planar Cubist space and Surrealist linearity, they expanded the resources of American art as virtually nothing had since the 1913 Armory Show.

Perhaps Still evolved more remarkably than any in view of his isolation in the remoteness of Washington state where he studied and taught from 1933 to 1941. There Regionalism should have been his métier. In practice he was far from its narrowminded horizons and his style after the mid-1930s reflected a shrewd understanding of his position vis-à-vis European developments, probably gleaned in part from reproductions in the French magazine *Cahiers d'Art*. After the early *Untitled ('Two Figures')* his imagery grew increasingly imaginative with suggestions of ritual in the detailing. One cause could well have been an interest in classical literature which pervaded his subsequent writings with their erudite diction and use of allegory. With a tutor who was a scholar in the field and a college library that included Frazer's *The Golden Bough* and Jane Harrison's anthropological study of ancient Greek myth, *Themis* (1912), Still's past encounter with the wasted Alberta prairies would have found an extraordinary equivalence in these books and their vivid symbols dealing with the fertility of the land. Amongst them stood awesome chthonic deities, living rocks, the sun or sky and elemental conflicts between life and nature. These elucidate the otherwise baffling pictorial elements that arose by the late 1930s, of which the remark that they were pictures 'of the Earth, the Damned and of the Recreated' (Rothko quoting Still in 1946) may be interpreted as a reminder. Thus the seminal canvas *1941-2-C* has a rearing brown and cliff-like silhouette, animated by crimson gashes, resembling a talismanic stone in *Themis* that symbolizes the earth. Its ominous bullet-like profile reappears at the base of several lithographs drawn in Richmond, Virginia, during 1943–45 which are fantasias upon 1930s themes including the struggle of light and darkness. *1938-N-No. 1* (once entitled *Totemic Fantasy*) perhaps casts a backward glance to Picasso's 1927 *Seated Woman* but is unique in its petrified chill, the aureole that throws the figure into relief and the

51
42

50 Ad Reinhardt *No. 30, 1938*

barren stalk it grasps which wavers upwards along the left side. Shapes
are also doubled and rhyme with one another in an uncanny fashion.
Still had therefore embarked on a twofold synthesis: private experiences were translated into universal terms – dark monoliths, bright
suns and prehensile limbs – boding human destiny within a hostile
cosmos and the symbols were then beaten flat to form planes jammed
together in a harsh post-Cubist framework. As these procedures had
few rivals in painting then, so the mythic allusions (if indeed they are
such) would predate their appearance in New York in the early 1940s.

69

51 Clyfford Still *1938-N-No. 1*

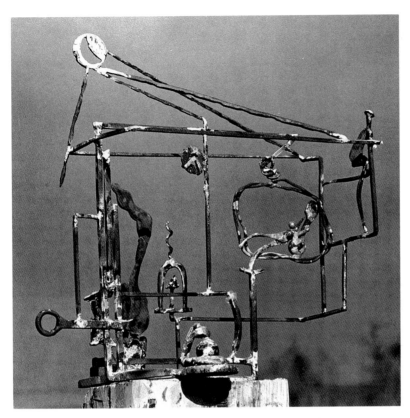

52 David Smith *Interior for Exterior* 1939

Still observed that he aimed at the time to resolve space and the figure, a process almost simultaneously paralleled in Smith's sculpture. Both at first reduced their subjects to schema which were then broken and reorganized as hybrid masses. Smith looked to Giacometti's *Woman with her Throat Cut* (1932) in *Structure of Arches* (1939) and replaced the splayed female body with zigzag interpenetrating angles. Contours next became important to both painter and sculptor. Some of Still's lithographs unexpectedly reversed shading and highlit passages so that all zones, 'empty' or solid, were alike equally 'active'. For Smith the counterpart lay in pieces like *Interior for Exterior* (1939) which employ steel rods at once to   52

53 Jackson Pollock *Panel with Four Designs c.* 1934–38

'draw' in space and imply solid volumes. Still's image of a wiry, ambiguous upright presence in *Oil on Canvas (1945)* would achieve a comparable breakthrough. The monoliths of *Saw Head* and *1938-N-No. 1* were approaching an art of spaces where line stretched into and energized its surroundings.

28
51

This disruption of a central anchor or focus held a special lure for Pollock because more than most he felt confined by the box-like space attendant upon it since the Renaissance and which Cubism had restructured without destroying altogether. Having progressed beyond the naive treatment of mass typified in *Going West*, Pollock's manner throughout the remainder of the 1930s gives the impression of representational conventions being pushed to the brink. He is in defiance of what a painting can reasonably contain. Despite or, rather, due to that spirit, Benton's example still loomed and he wrote in 1933 that the man had a 'huge job out in Indianapolis . . . two hundred running feet twelve feet high'. Soon, therefore, he wanted the mural's momentum – a quality linked to its declarative role as a public spectacle – for his own otherwise modest easel pictures. It explains the 'running' motion that courses through oils of the late 1930s such as

20

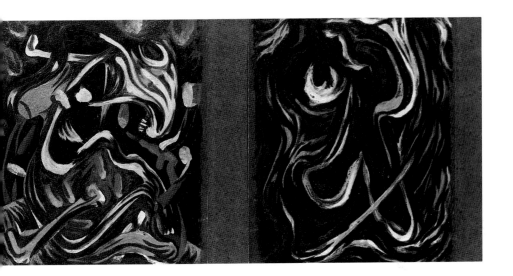

Panel with Four Designs (c. 1934–38) where the previous whirling   53
rhythms gather velocity, now as abstracted linear patterns largely
based upon figures. The difference is noteworthy. Before, the figure
was often dwarfed or absent; henceforth its gestures, traces and
convolutions in pictures such as *Naked Man with Knife* (c. 1938–41)   54
resemble violent retorts, as it were, to the forces that had oppressed his
initial works.

A major catalyst upon Pollock were the Mexican muralists Rivera,
Siqueiros and particularly Orozco whom he probably met when the
last did murals with Benton for the New School for Social Research in
Manhattan in 1930. Six years later he joined Siqueiros's Experimental
Workshop where enamel paints and unorthodox techniques including the use of sprayguns were being investigated. Above all, the
Mexicans had portrayed human turmoil on a heroic scale. Sketchbook
drawings from the end of the 1930s show that he took the lesson of   55
their murals, notably the shard-like patterns, dovetailed contours and
arabesques, and used it to overwhelm space. Amerindian calligraphy
and the Picasso of the *Guernica* years contributed much as well. Behind
each stood a new fixation with metamorphosis which is understand-

54 Jackson Pollock *Naked Man with Knife c.* 1938–41

55 Jackson Pollock,
sketchbook study,
c. 1938–39

able if we recall Pollock's initial concern with flux. The crisis of his graphics and paintings during 1938–41 is inseparable from their utter restiveness. One can discern the strands in the mélange but not unravel them: Picasso's bestial hybrids, ritual events from the allegories of the Mexicans and perhaps an even stranger dramaturgy drawing upon native Amerindian legends. They surely also merged in Pollock's own mind, part of the tumult whose formal consequences are an incessant, unresolved conflict between figure and ground on the canvas. Not unexpectedly, a personal crack-up ensued which led to hospitalization for alcoholism in 1937 followed by some five years of intermittent

75

psychiatric treatment. During its course Pollock became convinced that the sources of his art lay in the unconscious, a sincere enough conclusion that could still hardly have arisen without his sharing in the changed priorities of the New York avant-garde at a terrible crossroads in Western history.

CHAPTER FOUR

The Ideographic Picture

Notoriously, modern artists tend to conflate private crises with outside events and the Abstract Expressionists were no exception. Yet the Second World War, the Fall of Paris on 14 June 1940, Pearl Harbor and its entire dreadful aftermath justified this. Still and Smith alone participated in war industries; no others even came near combat due to various disabilities and so they shared the dubious privileges of the bystander: remote from physical conflict amongst the Greenwich Village intelligentsia, they could simultaneously view global chaos from a vantage point and still be affected by the spreading psychic malaise. 'In 1940', Newman recalled much later, 'some of us woke up to find ourselves without hope – to find that painting did not really exist.' Three years afterwards he participated with Rothko and Gottlieb in a letter-cum-statement to *The New York Times* heralding his incipient role as an adroit theoretician and self-styled philosopher. The latter's call for art to deal with the tragic belonged to an uncertain or even despairing mood which was a strong undercurrent in American culture then, as seen most clearly in Jewish novels like Saul Bellow's aptly titled *Dangling Man* (1944) and *The Victim* (1947), which explored the individual's psychology against the broader tragic sense of life. The grim or apocalyptic note about Abstract Expressionism through the 1940s similarly relates to a decade of cataclysm and historical fracture running from Pearl Harbor to the Cold War. Private traumas worsened the situation and besides Pollock's alcoholism, Still left his Richmond teaching post in an unrest of bitterness (1945), Gorky committed suicide (1948) and Guston, Rothko and Smith suffered depression or nervous collapses by the close of the decade.

So what subject-matter could respond to an increasingly bloodied modern history? To leaf through *The New York Times* for 13 June 1943 is a reminder that the now famous statement was almost a minor item in an issue dominated by over twenty pages of war reports. Against that context the ideas which Rothko and Gottlieb next expanded in an October WNYC radio broadcast assume an existential shading. They insisted upon the primacy of tragic content because 'in times of violence, personal predilections for niceties of colour and form seem irrelevant.'

Moments of horror frequently produce banal art and the controversy about how to treat them is older even than the eighteenth-century *Laocoön* debate (started by Gotthold Lessing's attack on Winckelmann's Neo-classicism), itself already revived in a 1940 *Partisan Review* article by Greenberg that Rothko and Gottlieb quite contradicted, as to whether aesthetic form should come before feeling. Though not silent in the face of Hiroshima or Auschwitz, painters hardly managed to express their enormity. No American Goya bore witness. Instead, the victims portrayed by George Biddle and Rico Lebrun, Shahn's rubble-strewn wastes and the aftermath fantasies of Philip Evergood and Henry Koerner are now understandably neglected on account of their academic or pedestrian allegorical vein. To avoid such pitfalls the Abstract Expressionists sought an imagery plumbing the psychological depths where momentous forces themselves originated.

One stimulus came with the arrival of several leading contemporary artists from abroad after the outbreak of war in Europe, including the grand theorist of Surrealism, André Breton, and some of its most innovative painters like André Masson, Ernst and the Chilean Matta Echaurren. Having already experimented with content or techniques meant to reveal the unconscious, they communicated their enthusiasms through personal contacts, direct or oblique, to the Americans. In 1941 Motherwell, for instance, travelled to Mexico with Matta and there met Wolfgang Paalen, a minor Surrealist who had an interest in the function of myth for ethnic and primitive peoples. Matta and Paalen also practised the Surrealist method of 'automatism' that entailed working rapidly and spontaneously as if to express, according to Breton, unconscious thought. Back in New York Motherwell transferred the impetus of this summary 'education in Surrealism' to his colleagues – if they were not learning of their own accord, as when Pollock around that date joined Matta, William Baziotes and Gerome Kamrowski (who subsequently left for Michigan) in group sessions where free association and the pouring of paint were explored. All in all, the moment was ripe for a younger generation to adapt these Surrealist concerns to their own purposes.

Another important link arose when Peggy Guggenheim, a collector who had herself fled the Nazi advance, opened the Art of This Century gallery in New York in 1942. Apart from Kandinsky,

Miró, Klee, Arp and Masson amongst many Europeans, she also searched out native talents that numbered Rothko, Gottlieb, Motherwell, Baziotes, Hofmann, Still and Pollock. Like the new wave of dealers who followed on her tracks, this was one of several signs that artistic impetus (and economic hegemony) had shifted during the War from Paris to New York. The melodramatic but natural perception then which supposed that if vanguard culture was to survive at all it would be on American soil furthered the sense of immanent self-importance. Without it the Abstract Expressionists would have been less steeled to break with Surrealism in certain key areas. Here there were to be no 'hand-painted dreams' in the style of Dali nor did automatism appear solely a matter of unconscious outpourings but rather, in Motherwell's words, a 'plastic weapon with which to invent new forms'. A common goal was perceived to be the mystery, violence and spontaneity associated with the modern experience on all its levels.

According to the 1943 *New York Times* statement, the tragic should aspire to be timeless *and* immediate. This last, seemingly paradoxical point suggests that the authors realized that timelessness is often a timely need and did not advocate mere escapism. Therefore, they wrote,

We favor the simple expression of the complex thought. We are for the large shape because it has the impact of the unequivocal. We wish to reassert the picture plane. We are for flat forms because they destroy illusion and reveal the truth.

Ostensibly these words rephrased well-worn avant-garde formulae reminiscent of Maurice Denis's famous injunction of 1890 stating that the 'idea' (now the 'complex thought') be expressed through the formal surface of a picture, itself echoing still older Neo-Platonic doctrines according to which meaning was locked up within the visual image; interestingly, both Rothko and Still studied or esteemed Plato. There is also a psychological dimension significant for the art ahead. Flatness and frontality have an imperative tense that forces us, so to speak, to confront them head-on. From there sprang the symmetry or repetitions that Rothko's *Slow Swirl at the Edge of the Sea* (1944) shares with Pollock's *Guardians of the Secret* (1943) and Motherwell's *Pancho Villa Dead and Alive* (1943). So too did the simplicity that Still, Gottlieb, Smith and Siskind pursued. The effect is of everything surplus being shorn away so that what remains is revelatory. A precedent existed in primitive art and several Abstract

57
59
66

Expressionists indeed looked to it, especially the striking symmetry or reductiveness of the exhibits at MoMA's 1941 'Indian Art of the United States' exhibition. Myth became their other major focus until by 1946 Rothko could refer to the 'small band of Myth Makers who have emerged here during the war'. Primitivism has a fairly obvious visual impact whereas myth does not and requires some explanation.

At root, myths are stories or legends, often of a primordial kind. They had already revitalized earlier twentieth-century literature and in Eliot's *The Waste Land*, Yeats's poems, Pound's *Cantos* and Joyce's *Ulysses* made a framework that added a universal or archaic dimension to the narratives of a troubled present, hence redeeming it *sub specie aeternitatis*. The fluid structures of Eliot and Joyce where fragments of disparate ages and cultures float as in a transparent stream were to be renewed in the oceanic drift epitomized by *Slow Swirl at the Edge of the Sea*. American novelists and literary critics had also begun to search for mythic designs in fiction during the War and the choreographer Martha Graham used them in her dances *Caves of the Heart* (1946) and

56 Adolph Gottlieb *Eyes of Oedipus* 1941

57 *right* Mark Rothko *Slow Swirl at the Edge of the Sea* 1944

Errand into the Maze (1947) to show the atavistic roots of all tragedy. But when used pictorially myth can still tend towards an illustrative approach which is far from 'immediate'; Rothko later implied this by denigrating Shahn, who favoured allegory, as 'essentially a journalist'. Instead, he explained in 1943 that his goal was 'dealing not with the particular anecdote, but rather with the Spirit of Myth, which is generic to all myths at all times.' This definition showed a further awareness of psychology.

First Freud and subsequently Jung proposed that myth articulated the deepest levels of experience and so voiced a universal language. By the late 1930s each had gained sufficient currency in America (like Joyce and Eliot) not to have to be studied minutely (as it is sometimes claimed Pollock did during the War) but instead absorbed broadly and intuitively. 'Psychology' to the Abstract Expressionist eye

81

represented a cornucopia of visionary and poetic images with an existential edge, especially since Jung claimed that myth issued from the same depths as art. This inner hinterland, the so-called 'collective unconscious', was supposedly common to all human beings, whether primitive or 'civilized'. Hence the 'archaic' look about the pictures of Rothko, Gottlieb, Pollock and Stamos was meant to cut through to inner truths. Moreover, the collective unconscious could only be known via mediators or 'archetypes': primal figures, symbols and the groupings associated with them that populate dreams and myths which resembled signs pointing towards things hidden and complex. These striking models of consciousness fired their imaginations.

56   In the 'pictographs' that Gottlieb began with *Eyes of Oedipus* (1941) figurative fragments, hieroglyphs and schematic forms are held by a rough gridwork in a flatly frontal manner meant, he explained, to 'kill the old three-dimensional space' that had characterized his previous mysteriously compartmentalized still-lifes painted with a veristic, Dali-inspired technique. By comparison the elements of the pictographs are metaphysical *signs* addressed to the viewer's mind rather than objects tangibly depicted. The logic at stake was to be reviewed in the exhibition 'The Ideographic Picture', held at the Betty Parsons Gallery in New York early in 1947, for which Newman wrote a catalogue essay stating that the ideograph 'by means of symbols, figures or hieroglyphics suggests the idea of an object without expressing its name'. Picto- and ideograph aimed that is, to bypass description and attain that portentous power beyond words which Jung thought characterized the genuine symbol. Mondrian, Klee, segmented designs by the Tlingit Indians and the Uruguayan painter Joaquín Torres-Garcia certainly foreshadowed Gottlieb's grids but a less jaded precedent says more about his outlook: namely the boxed constructions which Joseph Cornell started in the 1930s. By definition boxes and frames serve to store, so they are naturally associated with the passage of time and of contents hidden or set apart. Like Cornell's work, the pictographs seem to dredge some secret realm, their emblems hovering before us, the parts in a puzzle whose connecting thread is just beyond recall – except that rather than gentle musings the tone is traumatic, as the titles (*Evil Omen, Black Enigma* and so on) tell. *Eyes of Oedipus* renders its myth by a screen of blind stares. The

58 later and far more polished *Masquerade* (1945) shows that typical gathering of detail into a darkly hostile maze which has caused the series overall to be considered an abstract commentary on the neuroses of wartime.

82

58 Adolph Gottlieb *Masquerade* 1945

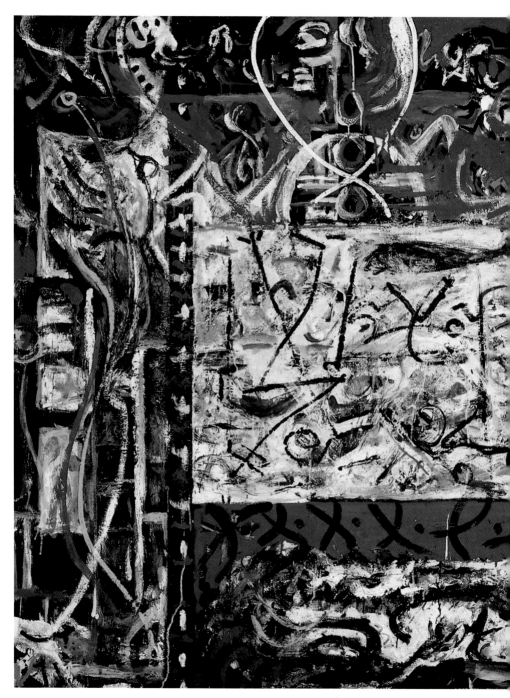

59 Jackson Pollock *Guardians of the Secret* 1943

60 Richard Pousette-Dart *Symphony No. 1, The Transcendental* 1942

Primitivist handling went together with the symbols of humankind's inward forces. One delved down into experience, the other into time so as to put us, wrote Gottlieb in 1945, 'at the beginning of seeing'. He had collected tribal masks as early as 1935 and the calculatedly primitive drawing accents the dry and timeworn cast of the pictographs that sometimes incorporate egg tempera and scratched lines. An extreme version of this archaism occurs in the early 1940s canvases of Richard Pousette-Dart, a rather neglected figure, perhaps because of a religious mysticism which separated him from the mainstream. Precocious in both size and drive, his aptly named 60 *Palimpsest* (1944) and *Symphony No. 1* (1942) possess encrusted layers akin to the aged textures of native Amerindian petroglyphs. Time and consciousness met more subtly in Rothko's technique by the mid-1940s where paleness, translucency and soft focus convey regression, especially if one remembers that on a far cruder plane superimposed effects or watery hazes were standard devices to convey flashbacks and reverie in the American cinema of these years. Once, Rothko's figures 57 had wavered in their trance-like states but in *Slow Swirl at the Edge of the Sea* the rhythms oscillate from a poised, gyrating calligraphy.

86

Historically, then, we can say that during the War and shortly after the Abstract Expressionists were borne on a tide of ideas which led them to assume, broadly speaking, that their work should be terser, allusive and pregnant. Aimed primarily at the eye and the mind it would therefore evade the distracting crutch of language. Pollock was quoted in 1944 as having remarked about *She Wolf* (1943) that it 'came into existence because I had to paint it. Any attempt on my part to say something about it, to attempt explanation of the inexplicable, could only destroy it.' Given such scattered sources, these ideas are better enumerated than treated like a detailed agenda. Their matrix was the usual mixture of studio and bar talk, casual reading and sensitivity to the intellectual stimuli of the day. Besides post-Freudian psychology, Plato and Surrealism it is worth noting the post-Jungians like Karl Kerényi who wrote about the indivisibility of thought and communication, the philosopher Suzanne Langer and her theory of the symbol as an emotive but non-verbal entity, and the New Criticism (influential too for Greenberg) which stressed an artwork's self-contained force or, as Cleanth Brooks wrote in *The Well-Wrought Urn* (1947), formed 'an experience rather than any mere statement about experience'. Nietzsche also found considerable favour and his assertion that art counters chaos and springs from primal roots was embellished by Rothko, Newman and Still.

Line served the new priorities well and no Abstract Expressionist failed to exploit it. Both Masson and Miró were in New York and their calligraphic genius could be seen at Pierre Matisse's and other galleries with Klee's in his MoMA retrospective of 1941. All three offered lessons in achieving more with less. From the bare stick figures in Motherwell's *Pancho Villa Dead and Alive* to the grating brushmarks of Pollock's mid-1940s canvases there is a new-found urgency. Pollock participated in 1944–45 at the printmaking studio of the British-born draughtsman Stanley William Hayter, who significantly wrote and spoke about the empathic power of line to make us re-live an event. Such essays by Newman as 'The First Man Was An Artist' of 1947 take up this observation and elaborate on the close bond between a manual gesture and its author. Quite independently Still had already equated the dynamics of a line with assertiveness in, or against, a surrounding space so that the white linear phantasm of several 1944– 45 paintings like *July-1945-R* (once given the title *Quicksilver*) slices 62 through their gloom as though it were midway between the semi-humanized, demonic lightning flashes of Harrison's *Themis* and the revelatory 'stroke' that he would mention in a letter of 1950. The

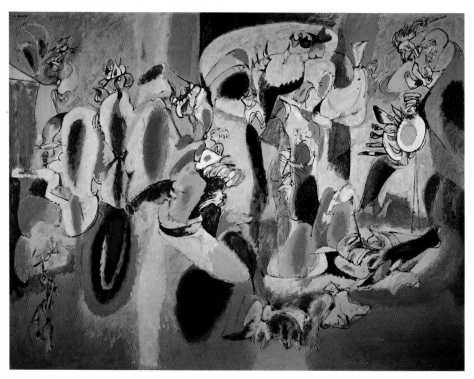

61 Arshile Gorky *The Liver Is the Cock's Comb* 1944

analogy of mark/space to vitality/void was to recur frequently and elsewhere Still reversed the duality so that a lean black slash presides over a bleak tan ground in, for instance, the Menil Collection's *Untitled* (1946).

The very act of drawing testifies to the universal language of line. That foundation seemed to promote the widespread penchant to limn mysterious scripts, unknown alphabets or other alternative visual systems to language. It occurred in Gottlieb's rebus-like pictographs with their many ciphers, the cabbalistic numerals in Pollock's *Male* 63 *and Female* (*c.* 1942) that crop up elsewhere throughout the mid 1940s, the hieroglyphic motifs of Smith's sculptures and the elegant tracery 64 akin to lettering and numbers that filled Tomlin's pictures until an untimely death in 1953 cut short his contribution. Even Siskind directed his lens onto subjects such as beached seaweed treated painstakingly enough for most of the themes mentioned so far to

62 Clyfford Still *July-1945-R*

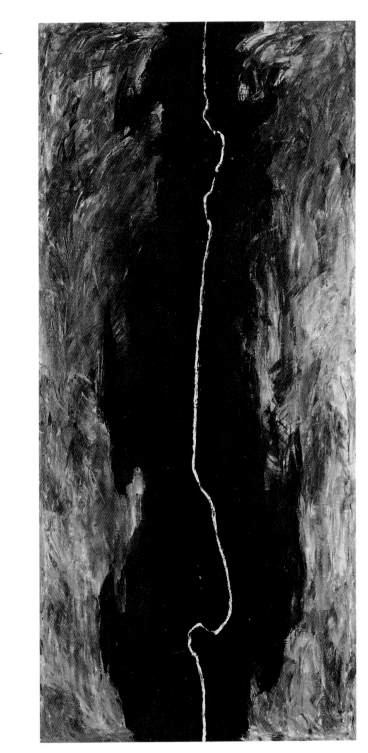

65   coalesce. *Martha's Vineyard (Seaweed) 2* (1943) reads multivalently as
tracing in the sand, a residual figure, a male sexual metaphor and an 'a'
(for Aaron?) sign.

Graphic effects in turn belonged to the more general and
momentous search for artistic means to match the rhetoric of
'universal', 'primal', 'archaic', 'symbolic' and like terms that flooded
the years of the ideographic picture when little magazines including
Possibilities (which ran to only one winter 1947 issue), *Tiger's Eye* and
Ideograph, as well as a spate of catalogue essays, revealingly made for
more published pronouncements than at any other time. According
to Newman writing in 1947, art worthy of its name should address
'life', 'man', 'nature', 'death' and 'tragedy' amongst other issues – an
ambitious list backed by some newly impressive pictorial
ammunition.

90

64 Bradley Walker
Tomlin *Number 9: In
Praise of Gertrude Stein*
1950

65 Aaron Siskind
*Martha's Vineyard
(Seaweed) 2* 1943

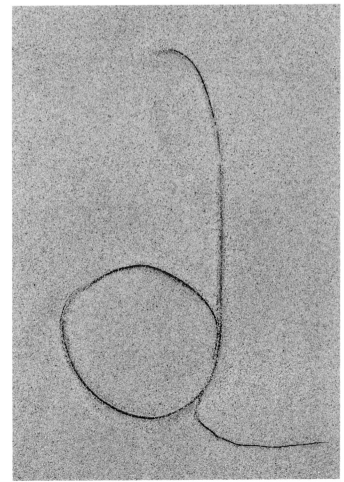

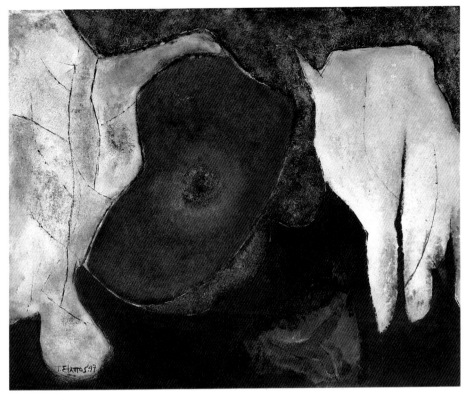

66 *above left* Robert Motherwell *Pancho Villa Dead and Alive* 1943

67 *below left* Jared French *The Sea* 1946

68 *above* Theodoros Stamos *Ancestral Myth* 1947

Symmetry, for instance, conveys a formidable air which in Motherwell's *Pancho Villa Dead and Alive* heightens the impact of a 66 'before-and-after' counterpoint whereby the bisected composition has vibrant patterning at the right confronted with blood-spattered grey planes on the left. That we almost seem privy to some sinister cross-section is an effect which recurs in Still's vicariously figurative masses outspread across the picture plane and in the initial paintings of Stamos which count amongst his best. Geological or botanic in their 68 delicate segmental structures, they express a current assumption probably gathered from readings in anthropology and biology which held that individual human beings recapitulated the processes of natural evolution. Hence to picture the innermost recesses of the natural world became a metaphor of life's origins, of its 'phylogeny'.

Paired male–female sentinels in Rothko's *Slow Swirl at the Edge of the Sea* and Pollock's *Male and Female* effectively represent the macrocosmic principles of nature. There was nothing unique here since similar hieratic polarities fascinated other American painters in the 1940s like

67 Jared French who were affected by Jungian theories. The divide between them and the Abstract Expressionists is equivalent to what separates literariness from the pictorial. The archetypes in several of

69 Rothko's 1945–46 watercolours are compelling not because of any staring pseudo-archaic postures but rather for how they act upon us slowly, temporal ebb and flow caught in textured washes where the figure is lost and rematerializes in the grain of the paper. As symmetry or linear forms appear instantly striking, so these veils imply mysteries locked within the picture surface.

Two concerns stemming from Surrealism returned to reinforce this encoding of the figure and what it symbolized into a less literal but

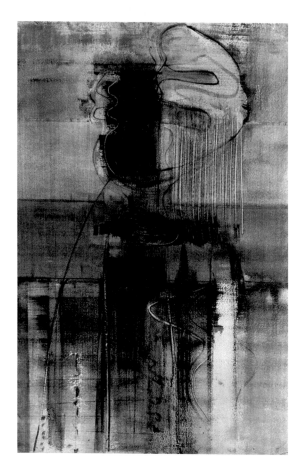

69 Mark Rothko *Untitled* 1945–46

70 Barnett Newman *The Death of Euclid* 1947

more provocative syntax: the totem and biomorphism. Totemic creatures as conceived by Masson, Miró and others essentially typified the Surrealist taste for fabulously bizarre personages, denizens of disturbed and disturbing levels of the psyche. Naturally that usage was not irrelevant in a fraught wartime context but the Abstract Expressionists also rediscovered the authentically primitivist vision of the totem as a hybrid between an animate presence and a sign, sometimes geometric or schematic in character, yet still embodying potent forces. To the Northwest Coast Indian, as Newman wrote in his 'Ideographic Picture' text, 'a shape was a living thing, a vehicle for an abstract thought-complex, a carrier of the awesome feelings he felt before the terror of the unknowable . . . [it was] therefore, real . . .'

In Newman's *The Command* (1946) and *The Death of Euclid* (1947) vertical shafts with a numinous and silent aura stand firm against dark or chaotic backgrounds while Still, perhaps from his past experiences

70

71 Aaron Siskind
Gloucester 16A, 1944

in the Northwest, certainly sought the drama of totemism. His Richmond studio was once described as having 'totems and strange images, both two- and three-dimensional, all around'. Livid eye-like dots or gashes stare out from amid tarry thickets of pigment in his mid-1940s canvases. Like the totem, these bridge an uncanny hinterland between the familiar and the unknown (and strongly vertical formats further emphasize their combative presence) which elsewhere explains the frequent suggestions at this time of 'watchers', sentinels and guardians. Images that return our gaze, sculpture that broods and bristles with hostility, the photograph where everything is fixed on a single plane – these alike had a special message in the years when malignant forces menaced humanity. In *Gloucester 16A* (1944) the schema are abstract yet physiognomic enough for Siskind to have later captioned it '. . . the blank eye, the hard profile, in a time of violence'.

71

It had become a commonplace by 1944 for American critics to voice the perception that Surrealism was ready for a marriage to the other major spearhead of European avant-garde art, abstraction. The

96

dealer Sidney Janis said as much in *Abstract and Surrealist Art in America*, published that year, and an exhibition was even organized by Guggenheim's adviser Howard Putzel in 1945 around this notion. Such opinions probably encouraged knowledgeable artists to mine Surrealism. Most of the Abstract Expressionists were anyway already predisposed to the poetic, suggestive content that it had given the modern tradition but disliked its fanciful excesses. Instead their priority was to find 'a pictorial equivalent for man's new knowledge and consciousness of his more complex inner self' (Rothko, 1945). Surrealist biomorphism offered the ideal means because, as the very word (*bio*, life and *morphe*, form) suggests, it could intimate living presences through abstract organic curves alone. At first Rothko's portrayals of evolving sentience produced the assembly of plant, animal, and geometric parts in *The Syrian Bull* (1943). Once he had 72 mastered a biomorphic repertoire shortly afterwards, the twist of a volute summarized an entire organism. Other variants ranged from Pollock's relatively coarse ovoids to Gorky's hypersensitive ones and even de Kooning, who mostly kept apart from Surrealism, broke down his previous protagonists into biomorphic planes. Between *Seated Figure* (1939) and *Pink Angels* (1945) specifics recede into the

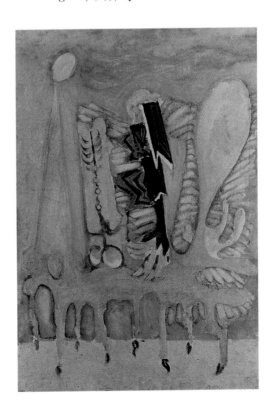

72 Mark Rothko *The Syrian Bull* 1943

threshing pulse of contours. In sum, biomorphism made for visual economy, enabling the leap from figuration to abstraction that dominates the 1940s.

Yet the passage of the decade looks clearer in hindsight than it actually was then and Smith's sculpture attests to this phase as a stylistic and ideological melting-pot. Embittered at spending two years in the wartime industry of welding tanks and locomotives, he fashioned the various 'spectres' of 1944–46 which personify the sinister spirit of the age comparably to Max Ernst's rapacious *Hordes* (1920s) and *The Angel of Hearth and Home* (1937). Mechanistic detailing, often from found objects, invokes weaponry while the phallic imagery cuts deeper still, a physical reminder of the aggressive side to sexuality. No timeless theme could have been more topical and besides Smith's invention of strange rapacious cannon–phallus hybrids (as in *Atrocity*, 1943) there was the obsession with eros in Graham's dances, Pollock's pregnant and explosive effects, frequent encounters of thrusting elements against open ones and Motherwell's explorations of sex and mortality. In death his Pancho Villa lacks genitalia.

The motif of airborne predators also located political trauma in genetic stirrings since it straddled pre-history as well as the wartorn skies of Europe and Hiroshima. Smith and others frequented the

73

73 *left* David
Smith *War
Spectre* 1944

74 David Smith
Widow's Lament
1942

American Museum of Natural History whose birdlike fossils caught
their attention, atavisms of the violence still at large under a
technological guise. The sculptors Theodore Roszak and Herbert
Ferber emulated these monstrous avian types from the late 1940s
onwards and Smith spawned a race of hybrids out of them whose
hovering skeletal profiles evolved from *Jurassic Bird* (1945) through
Spectre of Profit (1946) to some of the *Agricolas* (1952–59).

In trying to pack in as many meanings as possible Smith literally
arrived at composite objects, physical equivalents to the portmanteau
words and stream of consciousness that he admired, as did Pollock, in
James Joyce. Into that category fall the hermetic containers like
Reliquary House (1945), inspired by Giacometti's *The Palace at 4 a.m.*
(1933) and ancient reliquary boxes, the multi-partite landscapes
(*Landscape with Strata*, 1946) and various totemic pieces of which the
little *Widow's Lament* (1942) is a herald. Freud's *Totem and Taboo*   74
(1913) was known to Smith and this sculpture recalls a fetish except for
being more mercurial than the typical Surrealist prototype. Its frame
(which was most practicably cast in bronze) reads as a droll creature
with ears and feet, a picture plane for the action within, and an outsize
head whose welded steel 'thoughts' secreted in little boxes, though
quite abstract, received such autobiographical titles as 'knots of

adolescence' and 'sorrow'. Smith later termed these symbolic elements 'glyphs'. Though crudely and in miniature, *Widow's Lament* combines an anthropomorph's quizzical air with the clipped formality of an object, just as it alternates between a frontal plane and recessive ones. All these qualities were to pervade the sculpture ahead.

But despite Smith's inventiveness his rendering too often lagged behind his inspiration, a symptom of the cerebral approach inseparable from the ideographic picture endeavour itself and elsewhere responsible for the meagre appearance of certain Gottlieb pictographs and Newman's first surviving efforts in crayon and mixed media from 1944–47. This is the problem that novel subject-matter creates and it must ultimately be tackled not in theory but through the working process. Probably more than anyone, Pollock 'thought' pictorially – which explains his special intensity (and one that encompassed many failures too) throughout the early and mid-1940s. Commentators who maintain that he amassed an elaborate scenario of Jungian themes miss this point, for even the therapy (1939–*c.* 1942) under two psychoanalysts of that persuasion surely encouraged his intuition that innermost feelings were more powerfully externalized in images than words. Pollock's outpouring of symbols – bestial, sexual, geometric – was knowingly oracular and not often organized so as to relate any fully coherent narrative.

Shortly after *Naked Man with Knife* (*c.* 1938–41) Pollock destroyed the last vestiges of naturalistic space and did so through a new weightiness in the handling of pigment which makes the ovoid and elliptic shapes of *Bird*, *Composition with Masked Forms* and *White Horizontal*, all probably completed around 1941, appear to lie on top of each other or else to be submerged beneath a dense crust. Now that a shallow armature had gone, activity could be concentrated upon or even seemingly within surfaces teeming with incident. Sometimes he experimented with tactile substances like sand in *Bird* and plaster in *Wounded Animal* (1943), continuing this throughout the decade. Otherwise, from *Male and Female* onwards his actual deployment of oil paint acquired a life of its own. The first outcome was the great sequence of canvases all executed, remarkably, in or around 1943, that includes *Male and Female* itself, *She Wolf*, *Guardians of the Secret*, *Pasiphaë* and the rather different *Mural* (1943–44) commissioned by Guggenheim for her townhouse. For sheer coruscating vigour these represented a latter-day *Rite of Spring* to American painting. Theirs is the barbarism that unlocks future possibilities as it despatches a moribund present, in this case the fussiness to which Ernst, Masson and

59
75

late Surrealism in general had declined. In de Kooning's famous phrase, Pollock 'broke the ice'.

Unique and hard to fathom is the way Pollock churned myriad traces of his memories, enthusiasms and private fixations together with an approach geared to unrelenting spontaneity. On one hand, in *Guardians of the Secret* alone we find references to Picasso and his *Three Musicians* which show that he still regarded the European master as both rival and inspiration; more autobiographical details, like the red rooster (near the top centre) and dog (along the lower edge) which are hardly untoward for someone brought up on farms and with a well-known love of animals; and a taste for ethnology that suggests the composition was also advised by an 1894 photograph of hieratic Amerindian 'guardian' officials of a Knife Society. Moreover, the choice of format, a roughly 1 : 2 horizontal used here and in *Pasiphaë*, *Night Mist* (*c*. 1944) and *There Were Seven in Eight* (*c*. 1945) is by usage linked to the strongly declarative genres of mural and history painting.

On the other hand, a tremendous plasticity sweeps everything together so that blunt cursive gestures, filigree strokes, drips, splatters, numbers, broken scumbles and opaque overpainting run into one dancing optical medley. Even the 'Jungian' animus–anima figures of *Male and Female* are almost impossible to differentiate. The potency is in the allusiveness. Figures convert into ground, imagery becomes abstraction, and vice-versa. Perhaps here Pollock digested some metamorphic principles from perusing a 1943 edition of d'Arcy Thompson's classic *On Growth and Form* (1917), just as his symmetrical designs may acknowledge the geometric mandalas of the Amerindians. What counts far more is how each respectively continued a prior obsession with tumult and harmony. Indeed, that we cannot specify definitive meanings for the major early and mid-1940s pictures does not obviate their having a powerful 'content', an enigmatic core broadly shadowed forth. On that score the epic tone of ritual and cataclysm feels authentically mythic – in the tormented anatomies, masks and totems, the framing of the unknown in *Guardians* (whose 'secret' is the central indecipherable slab of calligraphy), and the pregnant nexus of *Pasiphaë* which are flung across the length of *Mural* with the frenzy of some maenadic procession. Its exceptional size seems to have afforded Pollock the glimpse of a line able to encompass great spaces and using the etcher's needle at Hayter's Atelier 17 in 1945 bore fruit in the arcing linearity of *There Were Seven in Eight*. Yet his painterly skills were not quite ready

75 Jackson Pollock *Mural* 1943–44

to integrate that line with colour and a vestigial symbolism. To do so needed an apprenticeship of a length that by then only Gorky had served.

Once the Depression had receded Gorky's fortunes brightened with a modest retrospective at the San Francisco Museum of Art in 1941 when he also married Agnes Magruder, followed by opportunities to reside and work in the country. In the summer of 1942 he stayed at a friend's in rural Connecticut and then with Agnes' parents at their Virginia farm in 1943 and '44. Artistic connections burgeoned as he met Matta in 1941 and Breton three years later. Also decisive was his shift away from Picasso's guiding influence to a study of the earlier Kandinsky and a deeper knowledge of Armenian culture.

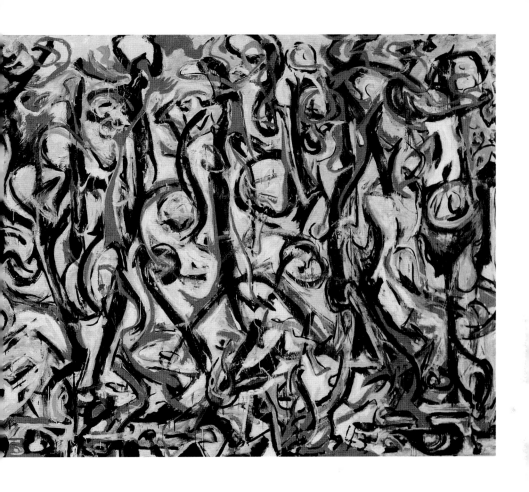

The discovery of an American outdoors that touched on Gorky's memories of the Armenian lowlands made for a psychological rapprochement with his pastoral childhood world. In graphics and then canvases which grew from days spent in the Connecticut and Virginia meadows he fused a scrutiny of flora and fauna with Surrealist biomorphism as if nature and artifice were no longer separable. They prove more fantastic than anything seen yet too vivid to be altogether imaginary. *Waterfall* (*c*. 1943) probably refers to the   76
Housatonic river falls but by now reality was camouflaged to leave, as Gorky wrote in 1944, 'the pulsation of nature as it throbs'. Visceral contours and even overt male and female sexual organs (towards the lower left in *The Liver Is the Cock's Comb*, 1944) again enunciate a   61

delving into life's origins matched by a colloquy of sharp, straining or ruptured motifs against softer ones that brings a groundswell of violence. Matta had prompted Gorky to experiment with highly diluted paint and this afforded a new and much-needed 'breathing' quality to the leafy greens and muted reds of *Waterfall* until in the most seemingly improvised works that ensued, like *One Year the Milkweed* (1944), the liquid hues resemble secretions trickling from recesses within the composition to soak the canvas weave. Yet this spontaneity where forms now float in front of the picture plane was for the most part painstakingly crafted and *The Liver* . . . is in fact based on a meticulous drawing from the previous summer that helps to clarify its leaps in scale from the micro- to the macrocosmic. Great bursts of vermilion, golds and ultramarine attest to Gorky's understanding of Kandinsky and establish a space charged with action, passing from surface to depth, tactile yet impossible to enter on illusionistic terms. Allied to the newly ambitious dimensions, this synthesis must have looked to several fellow artists then like a signal for the future.

104

CHAPTER FIVE

The Process of Painting

Though the Abstract Expressionists always resisted a single collective identity based on style, theories or social ties, they came closest to an avant-garde nucleus between the end of the War and 1950–51. By then a complex network of friendships and acquaintances had meshed. Some began long before, like the meeting of Guston and Pollock at their Los Angeles high school in 1927; others arose late and casually as when Kline built a studio partition for Tomlin and Guston in 1949; or else passing contacts, like Rothko's with Still in Berkeley in 1943, matured into a deeper rapport. More superficial signs of cohesion were the popular meeting-places in Greenwich Village that included the Waldorf Cafeteria and then the Cedar Tavern. The Club, a loose-knit artists' discussion group, was likewise founded in 1949. A year earlier Still, Rothko, Motherwell, Newman, Baziotes and the *surréalisant* sculptor David Hare each played some part in establishing the Subjects of the Artist, a short-lived school intended to reaffirm meanings in abstract art. In 1947 Rosenberg edited with Motherwell the single issue of *Possibilities* magazine which contained statements by several painters and Smith. Another periodical featuring their work and views, *Tiger's Eye*, appeared then and ran through nine issues.

Interest from dealers, critics and the media also exerted an external shaping influence. The *New Yorker* critic Robert Coates's description of Hofmann's paintings as belonging to 'abstract expressionism' was merely one of several attempts to label what appeared a new tendency. Given America's postwar prosperity compared with the economic and cultural exhaustion of Europe, its art market could be expected to capitalize on these circumstances and once Guggenheim returned to Venice in 1947 her role was more than fulfilled by the ambitious younger dealers Betty Parsons, Charles Egan and Samuel Kootz. Their New York galleries showed every major figure, from Motherwell at Kootz in 1946 to Krasner with Parsons in 1951, plus solo débuts for Siskind (1947) and de Kooning (1948) under Egan, while Smith exhibited at Marion Willard's gallery. Though support from public institutions lagged slightly behind, MoMA's '15 Americans' of 1952 (incorporating Pollock, Rothko and Still) announced the rise of high-level policies which would gain international fame for the movement by the end of the decade. On the whole the promotion of Abstract Expressionism entailed its stereotyping. It could hardly have been otherwise in the climate of the Truman and Eisenhower years.

America moved so far rightward after the Second World War that the 1945–60 era has been called 'The American Inquisition' and a time of 'The Great Fear' when conformity reigned, hysteria over the supposed threat of Communism was pandemic and surveillance or repression pervaded the fabric of culture. McCarthyism and the Cold War represented only the most visible symptoms of this far subtler totalitarianism than Russia's, which the novelist Ken Kesey symbolized retrospectively as the authoritarian insane asylum of *One Flew Over the Cuckoo's Nest* (1962). Furthermore, although contemporary liberals such as the Columbia University philosopher Sidney Hook and Arthur Schlesinger Jr in his *The Vital Center* (1949) purportedly denounced extremism, their rhetoric served to mask the dominant and itself extreme conservative ethos; Hook's willingness to side with McCarthy's denial of civil liberties was but one of many traits that put this 'liberalism' under quotation marks.

Controversy still surrounds the reading of Abstract Expressionism against this reactionary context. Neither an obviously partisan nor a monolithic response, it has subtle yet pervasive features calculated to transcend and contravene the political tenor of the times. We might expect this from the stances of the creators themselves. On personal terms they felt beleaguered, at odds with the establishment, or both, and as opposed to some of their earliest supporters, such as erstwhile leftist intellectuals like Greenberg, no evidence has yet associated them with Cold War ideals. Instead, Gorky deplored America's 'commercial philistinism' and inhumanity while Reinhardt risked contributing to an openly Communist publication as late as 1947 when Motherwell and Rosenberg alluded in *Possibilities* to how 'the deadly political situation exerts an enormous pressure'. Open dissent had become impractical and Still acknowledged this with a notion of art as a kind of guerilla warfare. Smith's leftist beliefs can be gauged by his declared identification in 1948 with 'working men' and Local 2054 United Steel Workers of America. This came a year after the repressive anti-union legislation of the Taft–Hartley Act. Both Newman and de Kooning made damning remarks about their country's atom bomb (when it was almost ubiquitously praised) and in 1948 the former was challenged to explain the meaning of one of his works to the world. If properly read, Newman answered, 'it would mean the end of all state capitalism'. To discover Cold War 'liberal' ethics behind such positions, as Serge Guilbaut and others have done, seems at best mistaken.

What does belong more to the moment is their turning inwards upon the processes of making art. Introversion had become commonplace by then as many writers and intellectuals retreated from the alarming or hostile political scene. A penchant for fantasy arose in the Southern Gothic novels of Eudora Welty and Truman Capote as well as in the arcane dreamlike compositions painted by Edwin Dickinson, Jared French, John Wilde and Henry Koerner. Concurrently a spectrum of existential issues involving selfhood, isolation and psychic malaise came to prominence. Yet whether in the fiction of Bellow, Malamud and Salinger, the early poetry by Roethke and Lowell, or the drily precise pictorial idioms of Andrew Wyeth, Bernard Perlin,   114, 100 George Tooker and Paul Cadmus, these again proved stylistically conservative.

Against these tendencies Abstract Expressionism effected a bold synthesis. It combined existential content and innovatory handling without a retreat into the ivory tower of form-for-form's-sake. Instead such developments of the later 1940s as very large formats, stark or saturated colour and a stress on the medium itself were ways to engage the spectator and even provoke a gut reaction. This was highly extreme art when the dangers of extremism – political and aesthetic – were widely and loudly decried.

Even the withdrawal to the solitudes of studio and countryside (Gorky went to rural Virginia and Connecticut, Pollock moved to a Long Island farmhouse in 1945, and Smith and Guston settled in upstate New York) had a double edge. There they could attain a stylistic audacity that left most contemporary realisms looking artificial and out of date. In the urbanism of Manhattan de Kooning and Kline found a similar intensity which also gripped Siskind's work as he alternated between there and Chicago with one interlude in remote Arizona in 1949. To create outside or at the edge of society during the Cold War provided an escape from consensus and conformity. Furthermore, an outburst of anti-modernism erupted during 1947–49. As *Life* carefully derided Pollock's methods, the Boston Institute of Modern Art switched its titular 'modern' to 'contemporary' and Senator George Dondero denounced non-academic twentieth-century painting as Communist subversion, so abstraction once again acquired the radical aura that it had held for a previous generation. Its originality now, however, was centred upon the Abstract Expressionists' physical exploitation of their materials.

At least since the famed passage in Leonardo's *Treatise on Painting* (first published in 1651) urging the discovery of subjects in random stains on walls, inspiration has been linked to directness and methods to transform felt experience into visual fact. In part the course of Western painting itself entails changing conventions to meet this end, from the control of illusionism in, say, Van Eyck, where the picture plane approximates a window (and thus offers instant access to the depicted scene) to the very different instantaneity of Monet which depends more on the freshness of painterly mark-making. Both worlds are vividly felt but how we apprehend that vividness depends on the rules whereby vision is reorganized upon a flat surface. For another analogy we might compare a name printed in Gothic lettering to one impetuously signed: the latter bears an especially close relation to its maker of a kind that semioticians call 'indexical' and has ambiguities and a pulse absent from the formalized Gothic script. Magnified to historical proportions, it was an analogous changeover that happened during the 1940s. The mimetic rendition of symbols (early 1940s) was phased into stark signs (mid-1940s) and eventually the indexical registering of traces (later 1940s). This progression was clearest in painting (though always mutable and its successive stages merged) but despite the technical obstacles to such directness in sculpture, Smith's attitude changed until by the early 1950s his erstwhile graphic symbolism and solid cast shapes modulated to the subtle forcefulness of the welded steel line or plane suspended in space. Equally, Siskind's photographs tended to replace objects with shadows, imprints, outbursts and other indexical effects. Since everything in the transition just described hinges upon those points where the artist's actions encounter our response – namely the picture plane and surface – their role was also transformed until Pollock's 1947–50 paintings centrifugally explode a hitherto shallow space and in de Kooning's *Excavation* terrific pressures bear down upon the contents of the image. Here the belief that a painting (or indeed a sculpture or photograph) had, in Pollock's phrase from 1947, 'a life of its own' that would 'come through' via the handling of materials bulked large because it spoke for a greater confidence in the power of the medium to embody messages. Motherwell put this succinctly in a comment on Pollock's 1944 show at Art of This Century: 'His principal problem is to discover what his true subject is. And since

124

84

77 Clyfford Still
Untitled 1946

painting is his thought's medium, the resolution must grow out of the process of painting itself.'

Probably even before Pollock, Still perfected the nakedly physical involvement in process that Motherwell foresaw. His 1946 *Untitled* 77 has the mastery of touch that fuses every knife-stroke, each colour chosen from an earth-toned palette, into an organic mosaic of pigment. It builds upon much earlier compositional types where twin protagonists, sometimes intertwined (as in '*Two Figures*') though here 25 separate, stand against a background. Only now the duality is pared to two snaking verticals landlocked in a fastness of umbers and sienna. The 'life' of the whole (also a favourite metaphor of Still's) resides in the ridges, smears and fissures of paint which catch the light. This erodes distinctions between figure and ground although the tonal contrasts emphasize them. The resultant space, if that word justly describes a flat yet manifold surface, exudes tension. We want to penetrate its inscrutable structuring but are prevented by the sheer tactility. The same happens in such 1946 Pollocks as *Eyes in the Heat.* 94 Surrealist automatism is usually given credit for this activated sense of

78 Mark Rothko
Number 18 c. 1948

touch but the difference between its theory and practice needs some mention. Though Breton defined automatism as working without conscious control the Surrealists scarcely went that far in reality. Pollock almost did after 1946 yet even he would insist that the flow of paint was ultimately regulated. Since he and others sought to represent states of consciousness rather than the unconscious itself, automatism served more as an instrument to add calculated elements of chance, spontaneity and flux.

Rothko's idiom illustrates the stages of assimilating automatism. During 1946 it grew lusher and the curves in *Aquatic Drama* are more

79 Barnett Newman *Untitled* 1947

ample than those of *Slow Swirl at the Edge of the Sea*, the calligraphy less pre-formed because loosened by the momentum of the brush. That degree of atmosphere which he had best realized in watercolours is at last admirably transposed to oils. Next the surface accommodates various levels of signification. In the metamorphic haze of *Number 18* (*c*. 1948), so akin to Gorky (compare his 1947 *Agony*), colour patches and other fleeting marks imply biological evolution as they congeal here and there into amoebae. The processes of life and of painting are therefore equated in a quintessential Abstract Expressionist metaphor. Already Newman had broached it in small mixed media works,

78
87

begun in 1944 after a four-year hiatus, that delve a similar brew, of genesis paralleled in the hand's rapid tracings. Their titles summon myths of creation and death. He explained: 'My idea was that with an automatic move you could create a world.' Slowly the biomorphs and spermatozoa regressed to the random textures, blots and automatic incidents in *Genetic Moment* and *Death of Euclid* (both 1947) and then, further abstracted, to the freely brushed inkiness of his 1945–47 graphics. Judging from Newman's testimony, these passages symbolize the entropy of nature and oppose more luminous or purposeful uprights which anticipate the single defiant vertical of *Onement I* of 1948.

70
79

121

Now the point to observe in advance is that most of the purportedly sudden 'breakthroughs' in the late 1940s and thereafter were as much climaxes to a longstanding or shrewd manipulation of polarities. Newman's dialectic of opposites, for instance, epitomized a phase when dualities were being articulated under novel patterns: automatism against structural order, geometry or disarray that threaten the organic fragment, and space neutralized by emphatic surfaces. Such are the terms behind disparate works like Newman's *Death of Euclid*, Still's *Untitled* (1946), Pollock's *Eyes in the Heat* and Guston's *Porch II* – all except the Still from 1947.

Yet for some the dialectic meant a long-delayed reckoning with abstraction. As the decade wore on, Kline was most noticeably stuck between two worlds. On the one hand his urban scenes, interiors and portraits looked outmoded. On the other, they had little inward symbolism to fuel the abstracting process and make it more than a veneer, so that the 'synthetic' Cubist colour planes of *The Dancer* (1946) and its study – his first avowed step in this direction – just hang upon a figurative armature. Small graphics instead provided the sole format where his fidelity to an observed subject meshed with an impromptu freedom of touch. Insofar as Kline remained at a loss to push this combination further he still had to learn from Pollock and de Kooning before finding the nerve to raise his speedily blocked-in schema to an imposing scale.

81
80

De Kooning himself had already converted that problem into a source of fertile contradictions. The crucial *Pink Angels* (c. 1945) entangles the means and ends of representation, taking the female form as its vehicle. Compared to the relatively Picassoid *Summer Couch* (1943), the nude (here seated rather than recumbent) appears closer still to compositional precedents in the Old Masters with a possible allusion to the far right-hand section of Titian's late *Diana*

89

88

112

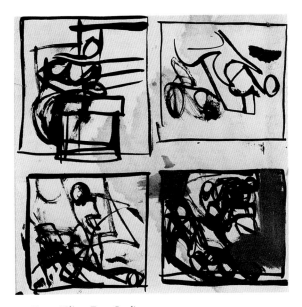

80 Franz Kline *Four Studies* 1945–47

81 Franz Kline, study for *The Dancer* 1946

surprised by Actaeon where the sinister goddess sits with upraised arm, an attendant to her right and a small dog below, which de Kooning parallels by a droll biomorph in the lower right corner. A shocking pink increases the hint of fleshly delights but automatic lines, most in charcoal, lacerate the anatomy. Ostensibly they model and shade the subject; perceptually they are intruders and so read as tokens of the painter's own exacerbation. In these violent indexical effects which fracture the iconography *Pink Angels* foretells what was in store until de Kooning suspended each extreme with *Woman I* (1950–52).

Over a similar timespan Motherwell translated polarities into style through a sort of aesthetic binomial method. Elements that he associated with the conscious (straight lines, designed shapes, abstraction) confront those allied to the unconscious (soft edges, obscured

113

82 Robert Motherwell *At Five in the Afternoon* 1949

shapes, automatism). Effectually he therefore paired the rectilinear concept of *The Little Spanish Prison* with the freewheeling collage principles and figurative curves from *Pancho Villa Dead and Alive* in
82   *Mallarmé's Swan* (1944) and *Western Air* (1946–47). With *At Five in the Afternoon* (1949), whose title refers to a death-haunted poem by the Spaniard Federico García Lorca, the dialectic froze into a sequence of black pillars that abut – and oppress – roughly painted ovoids. As a visual shorthand for an entire complex of antitheses (life/death, expansion/confinement and so on) he had found the germ of the grandiose *Spanish Elegies* series.

    To integrate extremes in photography and sculpture required a special skill owing to the inherent rigour of their laws. Around 1947 Siskind brought fragments together in the same shot as if they might be partners in a strange meeting. Later he termed two such couplings
83, 84   'conversations' and three, 'trinities'. In *New York I* (1947) and *Chicago*

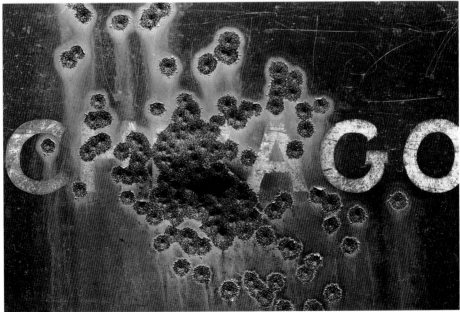

83 *top* Aaron Siskind *New York I, 1947*

84 Aaron Siskind *Chicago (Auto Graveyard) 3, 1948*

(Auto Graveyard) 3 (1948) impersonal signs like the arrow, background divisions and letters, encounter residual life in the
efflorescences of decay and graffiti. Other contemporary prints –
most focus upon walls – scrutinize textures or shadow play as
metaphors for unseen action and are so severely framed as to press the
medium's innermost nerve, its Midas touch that converts everything
to the prison of a flat rectangle.

   Whereas Siskind could exploit the thrift of the camera's reducing
lens, Smith had to tackle his own embarrassment of riches since by the
War's end he was making the naturalistic cast bronze *Spectre Riding the
Golden Ass*, the sparse frontal *Steel Drawing* based on Picasso's 1920s
dot-and-line designs and the intricate, symbol-laden tableau that is
Home of the Welder (all 1945). How to blend these modes in single
constructions? Much of his activity into the early 1950s addresses the
task. Found objects and steel from the stockpile gradually supplanted

86 David Smith *The Letter*
1950

the earlier intricate forgings as acetylene and subsequently arc welding
became his most direct tools.

   Sculptures from the transitional phase, notably *Oculus* (1947), *Royal*   85
Incubator (1949) and *Blackburn: Song of an Irish Blacksmith* (1949–50),
consist of disparate parts, including metal sheets and linear cage-work,
compiled with a nimbleness reminiscent of collage. The base of *Oculus*
is a columnar pedestal inviting an all-round view even though the
composition above is planar and manages to evoke landscape, a
sentinel and an uplifted still-life. Here Smith moved abreast of Siskind
and those painters whose abbreviated imagery sparked a train of
associations. The finest early 1950s' efforts exalt that open-ended look.
Such is *The Letter* (1950) which adopts the bare signs already seen in   86
Siskind and Motherwell for its tracery of characters that articulate
voids against solid. Beautifully 'written' in steel to conciliate Smith's
future wife Jean Freas after a quarrel, some of the object–symbols

117

came from a hardware store, others resemble a cursive script at top and bottom and several distil sexual imagery from the past. Overall they subtly continue, penetrate or recede from the plane of the pedestal-cum-frame. This and comparably hieroglyphic pieces such as *24 Greek Y's* (1950) and the large *The Banquet* (1951) breathe the economy that follows when vision and design are united. With them Smith had resolved the difficult interim years that every other major artist, bar one, saw to a close. Gorky was the exception.

Something cruelly apt surrounds the catastrophes that started when a fire destroyed Gorky's studio and its contents in January 1946, followed by cancer, a car accident, impotence and at last suicide by hanging on 21 July 1948. It was as though his tendency to romanticize an already dramatic existence turned into self-fulfilling prophecy. Indeed, the ecstasies of *The Liver* . . . had already settled to a deeper gravity in the almost grisaille *Diary of a Seducer* (1945) that corresponds with his rejection of Surrealism's obsession with the unconscious. Sensing how the lines of the ultra-fine signwriter's brush (to which de Kooning had alerted him) could carry a certain impulse that we relate back to bodily rhythms, Gorky drew armatures in *The Betrothal* (1947) and *Agony* of an intolerable fragility and torsion. Colour reinforced the pathos: either condensed to the sultriness of *Agony* or attenuated to exotic apricots, lilacs, sap green and tinted greys, its poetry was to be matched perhaps by Rothko alone of the Abstract Expressionists.

87

Research has uncovered an iconography behind the late paintings and evidently *Agony* is an interior with some central tortured being and another personage to its right. Others – many are series – evolved from domestic surroundings (*The Calendars*, 1946), landscape (*The Plow and the Song*, 1947) and events tinged by autobiography (*The Orators*, 1946–47, suggests an oration at his father's bier). Certainly the impression of a once recognizable world obscured within chromatic veils is a valid one because his shapes retain what Breton called a 'hybrid' character subsuming botanic, animal and human physiologies. So had he eventually discovered himself as a draughtsman or as a colourist? Both powers shine through *The Plow and the Song* only to be replaced by a plenitude of colour in *Agony* and *Dark Green Painting* (1948), the graphic cat's cradle of *Summation* (1947) and then the *alla prima Last Painting* (1948) whose brushwork conveys great velocity. Terminated in full flow, Gorky's career stood unresolved and the furthest exploration of the mine of possibilities opened up by his sudden, late zenith rested with successors.

87 Arshile Gorky *Agony* 1947

As it happened, the year before Gorky died saw Pollock's decisive maturation. Between then and 1950 he gathered up the key issues of the period with an imperiousness that must have drawn upon reserves of intuition. Significantly, the quickest to understand his feat tended either to be colleagues who could empathize with it or the rare critic like Greenberg who despite his dogmatism had a painter's eye *par excellence*. The latter hailed Pollock in 1949 as 'one of the most important painters of our age' and, for the former, Smith (according to Freas) simply spoke of 'the Number One boy'. A popular audience, stirred by the media, also naturally regarded him for better or worse as a figurehead to what otherwise appeared an irreducible 'movement'. The most curious aspect is that few were further from any glimpse of destiny or renewal than Pollock in 1946.

Trouble loomed as usual. True, Pollock had married the formidably protective Lee Krasner the previous October but his alcoholism worsened that winter, their newly bought farmhouse in The Springs, Long Island, was rundown and he stooped to borrowing two dollars from the local café owner. The 1945–46 graphics are sometimes better than oils like *Totem Lesson 2* or *The Blue Unconscious* which fail to reconcile drawing and planarity. Also, he had to paint in a relatively confined upstairs bedroom at first and notwithstanding other stresses several 1946 pictures betray the frenzy of someone whose available resources are at full stretch. The pressures manifest in *Eyes in the Heat* (1946) are outrageous. It is the crisis of *Naked Man with Knife*, of how to match spatial structure to content, all over again. Recurrent ellipses or the titular 'eyes', a favourite Surrealist symbol of the inner life, are sucked into the surface 'heat' which is a lather of such teeming incident that the easel dimensions appear inadequate. This canvas and *Sounds in the Grass: Shimmering Substance* (1946) approach chaos. One discerns Pollock packing more into them than his stabbing hand movements and the viscous impasto, sometimes straight from the tube, would carry. What ensued, to paraphrase him, grew naturally from a need – the need for a seamless flow between painter and painting.

Late in 1946 Pollock began to pour, drip and dribble oil, enamel and aluminium paint onto sized but unprimed canvas stretched on the studio floor. Tools included sticks, hardened brushes or, when pouring directly from the tin, his own arms. Vitally, this brought his entire body and not just the hand and wrist into play. As the weather got warmer into 1947 he moved to the barn which had more room and an inspirational view onto Accabonac Creek. Now although what Pollock created from then until around late 1950 was extraordinary the methods as such were not. Discoveries themselves matter little; how they take effect is all-important. Neither horizontal work surfaces nor the dripping of paint were novel: he himself observed that some Indian sand painters of the West had used the first, while he saw the second practised in Siqueiros's experimental workshop back in 1936, probably knew that Ernst and Miró had 'dripped' quite tactfully, and perhaps was further aware that Hofmann did pourings (in part) such as *Fantasia* during the early or mid-1940s (their exact dating is now uncertain). Though Hofmann's nearest approach to Surrealist automatism, it can also be argued that these conform to his assertion that the painter should find inspiration in his medium. There is a likelihood that this tenet filtered through to Pollock via Krasner or Greenberg. Whatever the case, *Fantasia* is not in the Pollock mould

88 *below* Titian *Diana
Surprised by Actaeon* (detail)
1556–59

89 *right* Willem de Kooning
Pink Angels c. 1945

because its dribbled line of white lacks the continuity which he would find for it. But in another sense Pollock's methods, or rather the frame of mind that nurtured them, had foundations broader than Hofmann's.

'Energy and motion made visible – memories arrested in space' was Pollock's simple but revelatory note that paraphrases the 1947–50 works and behind it stretches a tradition of seizing the transient that had flourished especially well in America. Eadweard Muybridge's famous images of frozen motion provided one early version of it from the 1880s and when the poet Hart Crane wrote in 1923 about Stieglitz's photographs,

> Speed is at the bottom of it all, the hundredth of a second caught so precisely that the motion is continued from the picture indefinitely: the moment made eternal

he might have been describing *No. 1A, 1948* or the Modern's *One (No. 31, 1950)*. Those linear maelstroms also contain something from   92

90 Skater, *Life* 1945, photographed by Gjon Mili

91 Hans Hofmann *Fantasia c.* 1943

92 *above right* Jackson Pollock *Number 1, 1948*

93 *right* Weegee *Coney Island, 4 p.m. July 28, 1940*

Pollock's slightly naive understanding of the modern age as epitomized by 'the airplane, the atom bomb, the radio' (1950), in short,
instantaneity and speeding wonders. Nor is it trivial to say that the
90 spirit of the 1945 photograph of the skater tracing her movements in
luminous lines adumbrates Pollock since he was far from aloof
towards an American popular culture of the 1930s and 1940s – think of
its design aesthetic – that equated modernity with directness,
dynamism, transparency and great sweeping lines. Sensitive as ever,
on the other hand, to the mechanics of fine art, he probably realized
too that Krasner's style by 1946 was more prescient than his in one
notable respect. From Mondrian's plus-and-minus compositions she
had learnt to splinter her rhythms into fragmentary touches spread
with almost equal emphasis over a series entitled *Little Images* that

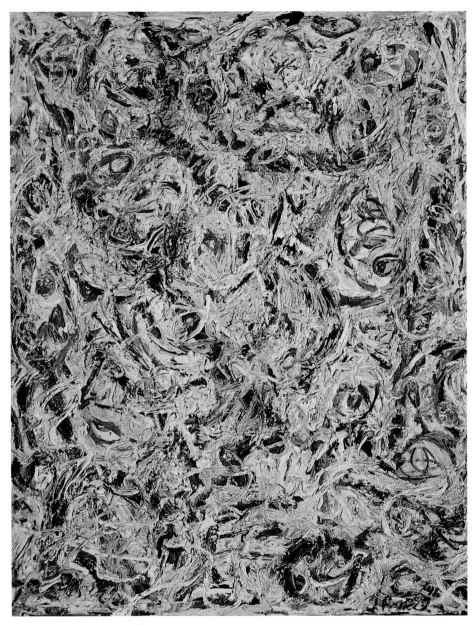

94 Jackson Pollock *Eyes in the Heat* 1946

95 Lee Krasner *Noon* 1947

began with such pictures as *Noon* (1947). This 'all-over' structure 95
makes the *Little Images* hypnotic in their own right and, given
Pollock's collaboration with Krasner in 1947 on two mosaic tables
that contained shards of numerous objects and substances, her
audacity must be acknowledged behind the atomized quality that he
attained.

The consequences of Pollock's new methods were vast, his account
of them in *Possibilities* lucid:

When I am *in* my painting, I'm not aware of what I'm doing. It is only after a
sort of 'get acquainted' period that I see what I have been about. I have no
fears about making changes, destroying the image, etc., because the painting
has a life of its own. I try to let it come through.

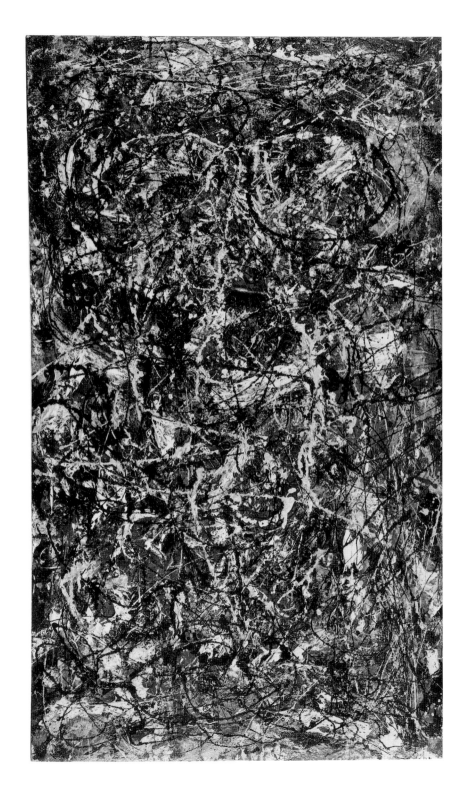

To be *in* the work – approaching the canvas on the floor from all four sides – Pollock had to increase its size until *No. 1A, 1948* met what he had envisaged in 1946 as a midway point between the easel picture and the mural. The 'big picture' was in vogue then anyway: MoMA mounted an exhibition on this theme in 1947 (which included Pollock's 1943 *Mural*) and Still in particular was already exploring the large format as a guarantor of immediacy. Historically the mural has epic connotations whereas one convention of the easel work is an intimacy engendered by the artist's touch or standpoint. The finest 1947–50 pictures retain both. Their drip technique enabled Pollock to expand his graphic talents to a magnitude that no pencil point, charcoal, etching needle or even brush-head could encompass. This is part of its indexical excitement, a kinaesthesia where the paint skeins endlessly switch course and tensile strength so that the mind's eye telescopes back and forth from the vivid surfaces to volatile gestures. 92

75

Pollock's emphasis on bodily gesture has spawned various theories and myths ranging from Rosenberg's 'The American Action Painters' essay (1952), which portrayed someone gripped by an almost mindless spontaneity, to recent claims that he was enacting a therapeutic ritual in the manner of a Navajo shaman. The truth is closer to hand. It was by then commonplace in New York artistic circles, as Matta recalled, to assume that direct gesturing was more powerful than verbal expression. Similar premises underlay both Graham's dance and the 'method' school of acting that developed from around 1947 onwards. Behind this extends a romantic assumption (immortalized in Yeats's line 'how can we know the dancer from the dance?') according to which art that is truly physical has an organic life beyond words. Secondly, the drip technique answered a need by co-ordinating thought, action, drawing and painting into a single process. Pollock's unusual abstinence from alcohol during 1947–50 signalled this state of integration whose corollary was the disappearance of the figurative or archetypal imagery that he had otherwise never quite abandoned. What happened to it remains debatable. Some initial drip paintings retain traces of that earlier febrile 'life' under an altered guise. Thus *Full Fathom Five* (1947) holds emblems from the realm of normal experience – nails, buttons, cigarettes – embedded in its sea-green swell. Thereafter 'life' gravitates mostly to the webbed labyrinths themselves, though other types of signification occur such as the handprints that mark the span of the upper reaches of *No. 1A, 1948* and *Lavender Mist*. Like the figural areas Pollock cut from the masonite ground of *Out of the Web* (1949), a composition perhaps otherwise 96

98

127

97 Jackson Pollock *Tondo* 1948

98 Jackson Pollock *Lavender Mist* 1950

headed for failure, this sudden emergence of recognizable phantasms in an abstract matrix is uncanny, as if further messages resided under the engulfing strands. They probably do not, yet the relentless layering does imply unfathomed mysteries or at least 'pressures' lurking underneath the superstructure. So much here encourages a leap of the imagination.

Yet little in the mainstream of Western art quite prepares the viewer to perceive *No. 1A, 1948, Lavender Mist, One (No. 31, 1950)* and

Autumn Rhythm (1950). A strain of calculated Americanness in Pollock might direct us to native precedents, even to the sensationalism of a Weegee photograph, for a foretaste of the reign of wonder exerted by such multitudinous incident held in a continuum. Or Joyce's *Ulysses* (the first unbowdlerized American edition had appeared in 1934) and especially Whitman's poems (Pollock owned copies of each) have a similar sweep, the likes of which Monet alone had glimpsed in his late *Nymphéas*, though these were scarcely known in New York at the

93

time. Never had painting been so far from the compositional hierarchies, perspective and figure–ground relations that go back to the Renaissance. In these liberated fields only the differing densities of line, no longer reading as contour anyway, imply depth gradations. But they do so along an absolutely frontal axis as if both were suspended in an eternal present. This is the magnetism inherent in the all-over design, its all-at-onceness which had already captivated Krasner, and Tobey and Morris Graves on the West Coast who were preoccupied with concepts of flux and infinity. Pollock's apocalyptic grandeur breaks with their minor-key Orientalism as well as the quietist or existential gloom that had become fashionable on both sides of the Atlantic.

Rather than limit Pollock's expressive range, the new approach widened it. After the crystalline upright *Phosphorescence* (1947) followed the fluent horizontal ($38\frac{1}{8} \times 189$ inches) of *No. 2, 1949* and the shot silkiness of *Lavender Mist* occupied the same year, 1950, as the muscular black-and-white *No. 32*. 'Classic' or 'classical' are the superlatives sometimes lavished upon this virtuosity (by William Rubin and Lawrence Alloway in particular) but the second epithet fits for a more profound reason. As applied to fifth-century BC Greek art, 'classical' denotes a peak when chaos was mastered and extremes balanced and it is this same poise about the 1947–50 images that allows them to reconcile contradictions. Empty of imagery, they feel intensely full; lacking overt references to nature, the organic patterns of growth nevertheless engulf us; rather monochromatic overall, strong and metallic hues shimmer through their interstices; heavy with the quiddity of paint, their space floats and dances in front of one's eyes. Pollock had also solved his oldest dilemma because although the microstructure of these images is violently disruptive his control over their macrocosm triumphs at the last and they remain too entire ever to divide. So *Tondo* (1948) gathers its testing format into perfect equilibrium and the tracery tends to loop back from the sides upon itself making an in-turned unity, or sometimes coheres into a vortex, or else attains the totality of a field.

Seventeen drip paintings were first publicly seen at Betty Parsons in January 1948, the show where de Kooning remarked that 'Jackson's broken the ice.' Less than three months later his own solo at Egan's caused a frisson second only to Pollock's with works that contemporaries again held to deal with the process of painting. At that moment their rawness seemingly expressed the same proto-existentialist stance responsible for the rhetoric of immediacy found in the artists' postwar

97

statements: from Newman's claim that they were engaged in 'a tragedy of action' (1945) through Gorky's avowal that he never finished a painting (1948) to Hofmann's denial of control (1950). Dicta spoken long before by Picasso amongst others, these were necessary myths to confront the same issue that in retrospect became de Kooning's real errand after *Pink Angels*: how can the inherently static artwork comply with lived experience? His reply over the next five years or so furnished further proof that to represent experiential values – immediacy, action, memory, violence – required not frenzy but the utmost craft. Once it was customary to accept Greenberg's remark that de Kooning aimed to marry painterliness onto the faceted infrastructure of 'analytical' Cubism. Now such a conclusion seems to miss a great deal.

Several reasons prompted de Kooning's reduction of his palette around 1946 to a dominant black or white. Visually it undermined tonal relations and so heightened the spatial netherworld of *Light in* 99 *August* and *Painting 1948* whose nearest counterparts are the nocturnal urban wallscapes of the artist's friend Siskind, especially in their high photographic finish that parallels the sinister gloss de Kooning achieved through enamel paints like Sapolin and Ripolin. One suspects that his muse was also the city. Since the Paris of Baudelaire it had been associated with precisely the swarming and fragmented phantasmagoria that inhabit the black-and-white works which in fact employ such sources as still-life objects, Picassoid biomorphs, lettering and architectural details to build a domain scarcely identifiable, as if refracted in a wilderness of mirrors. On night walks through what he called Manhattan's 'Byzantine city' de Kooning was accompanied by his friends Denby and Burckhardt. Their contemporary poems and, respectively, photographs, shed light on his compositions in that they condense vision into an allusive flux (Denby's phrase was 'a catastrophic perspective') where interior and exterior, human anat-omies and the textures of a wet sidewalk interact. This was also the heyday of the *film noir* (de Kooning was an avid cinema-goer), detective novels and Weegee's *Naked City* (1945): each treated the metropolis as a darkness fraught with violence, eroticism and unexpected reversals. If it is seen that the ambience of the black-and-white abstractions is essentially the New York inferno of Weegee, Cadmus's *Playground* (1948) and Perlin's *Orthodox Boys* (1948) then the 100 degree of de Kooning's avant-gardism is plain. Instead of their pedestrian treatment of life foundering in darkness or trapped by the urban tangle he located such traumas upon his scabrous surfaces.

101 Willem de Kooning *Excavation* 1950

99 *above left* Willem de Kooning *Light in August c.* 1946

100 *left* Bernard Perlin *Orthodox Boys* 1948

In *Town Square* and *Mailbox* (both 1948) a chalky pallor overcame the blacks and, despite a gathering all-over organization probably assimilated from Pollock, hominids emerged in the shape of schematic limbs, heads and a toothy grimace that returned above left of centre in *Excavation* (1950) which with *Attic* (1949) was the culmination of the 'white' series. The latter title and its presences in torment as though crushed by the depictive flatness – both reminiscent of the nightmarish painter's attic in Kafka's *The Trial* (1936) – probably owe some debt to the interiors of Beckmann who had a retrospective in 1948. Without any point of rest and pierced by shrill reds, blue and chrome yellow, these two canvases embody perhaps the ultimate expressions of ferocity in all painting. This illusion, because pigment cannot have volition nor acts exist on canvas, is conjured through disjunctions that evoke breaks in time (and stem from de Kooning's use of overlaps in his collages), a blurred facture akin to how the camera 'freezes' movement, and incessant ambiguities. Everywhere sharp drawing makes us discern figural profiles, rifts and likenesses. Yet everywhere brushwork reiterates a viscous surface maze: 'the texture of experience', de Kooning said, 'is prior to everything else.' We can enter it anywhere. Indeed, like the model text described by Roland Barthes as a multi-dimensional space where meanings clash, *Excavation* is a whirlpool of referents and signs. Here de Kooning also came to the threshold of a chromatic field and we must now turn to how others explored that most extreme pictorial phenomenon.

CHAPTER SIX

Being and Field

Time has confirmed the wariness of those in this book about how criticism would distort their endeavours. Whenever we distinguish between 'action painting' or 'gesturalism' and 'colour-field painting' it creates a division that they themselves never countenanced. Such slanted perspectives originated with the very critics who sought to define the movement. In the 1947–48 winter Rosenberg and, surprisingly, Greenberg wrote about them as if they were somehow romantic *peintres maudits* in absolute isolation. Gloom and doom were then popular in Europe and with America's disillusioned ex-Communists and 'liberals' as an escape from society into generalities about the human condition. Ironically, the artists had already mined this particular vein in the 1930s: Still's *'Two Figures'*, Guston's 25
Conspirators, Smith's *Saw Head*, Pollock's *Going West* and de 30, 28, 20
Kooning's *Man* preempt by a decade even the French 'realists' of the 35
aftermath of the Second World War who tried to portray the isolation and brutality of existence. By then the Americans had converted that early iconography into abstraction, or were about to do so. But this was just when Rosenberg and Greenberg pictured them as cut off from their past and heedless of contemporary culture. This set the pattern for future accounts which excised the continuing legacy of their earlier subject-matter, overlooked its relation to the present and created a vanguard who had retreated from there to the studio. That became the 'arena' of Rosenberg's American 'action painters' and three years afterwards Greenberg's '"American-Type" Painting' also eschewed talk of meaningful content and concentrated upon stylistic features. Its chosen ten were separated into a majority who fused painterliness onto Cubist space, Pollock as a bridge extending this to an all-over fragmentation, and another group (Still, Newman, Rothko) who advanced to homogeneous fields of colour. These stereotypes – indefinable images borne of action versus colour fields – steadily entered the literature until in Irving Sandler's impressive *Abstract Expressionism: The Triumph of American Painting* (1970) the division was codified.

102 Clyfford Still *1948-D*

Yet simply to look without prejudice undoes the neatness of labels.

119 So Still built the great field of *Painting 1952* from immensely 'gestural' marks. He, Rothko and Newman anyway meant their work to be as impassioned as any 'action' painting while many Pollocks and de Kooning's *Excavation* are really fields. Stylistic criteria alone would

121, 128 class Newman's *Onement I* and de Kooning's *Woman I* as antitheses and miss their dual manifestation of a central presence intended to galvanize our attention. Meyer Schapiro shrewdly sidestepped these

136

clichés when he noted in 1956 that overarching Rothko and Pollock stood a common search for an absolute, either of compulsive movement or colour, creating 'a powerful, immediate impact'. He saw the deeper unity that marks the climactic moment of the late 1940s and early 50s when former themes were regenerated at a visionary level: one where the spectator's act of perception was to be imbued with the emotions merely shown before as states of solitude, malaise, energy and so forth. Hence all argued that abstraction was more concrete than realism. 'It confronts you', said Pollock in 1950.

Since a recurrent preoccupation had been consciousness and its ambience, the pursuit of absolutes logically led towards the field which melds figure and ground into a totality or sets the viewer alone before its expanse. There was nothing divisive about who used fields; some Rothkos are less field-like than *Excavation*, for example. It is rather that several Abstract Expressionists exploited its emotive revelations of colour, scale and light the furthest. The evolution towards the field in 1946–50 took place when most Americans feared a third global conflict loomed and the radical few suspected their country in any case of descent into a dehumanized nightmare. This situation provided those struggles between awareness and chaos, death or conformity that are found in the contemporary writings of Norman Mailer, John Hawkes, Saul Bellow, Arthur Miller and Ralph Ellison. The same symbolic dualities occur in the paintings of Still, Rothko, Newman and Guston immediately prior to their resort to the field, like a core of expressionist matter about to undergo transformation.

Still's *Untitled (Oil on Paper)* (1943) is a last throwback to his 103 awesome 1930s personages and several titles (whoever originated them) in the 1946 show at Guggenheim's apparently referred to cycles of death and rebirth in the life of the earth mentioned in Harrison's *Themis*. A gaunt female presence (note the circular breast-like detail) is engulfed by rising black lines that resemble outgrowths, a thicket sprung from the single stalk held in *1938-N-No. 1*. As befits a small study, the means are simple with brighter touches like the face with its two red eye dots. In corresponding oils the figurative aspect receded, with an emphasis on opaque versus luminous tones in *Untitled 1946* and 77 *1946-No. 1* (Des Moines Art Center) where the earthy hues encroach upon glowing fissures and verticals that Still was quoted in a 1948 magazine review as calling 'living forms springing from the ground'. Texture adds its vividness, changing from matt to glossy, thin to encrusted. The outcome of subsuming previously skeletal figures,

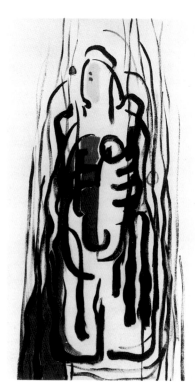

103 Clyfford Still *Untitled (Oil on Paper)* 1943

bodily details and space into an abstract topography was a tangled realm with 'life' – glints of untoward and hence premonitory colours such as burnt orange, alizarin and purples – lurking within it. Once darkness or, more rarely, a glaring acid yellow, indigo or crimson spread to a field-like magnitude the onlooker no longer faces *depictions* of extreme situations. Instead these are painted terrains to be reckoned with, their signifiers more substantive than the signified. The grimmest exude a *stimmung* otherwise familiar in circumstances when little can be seen but much can be sensed and Still would have known such moments on the barren prairies, especially at night. Perhaps these distant memories were a spur to the works' attainment of an 'iconic' state where the image partly embodies that to which it refers. This helps explain his observation in 1950 that they were 'not paintings in the usual sense. They are life and death merging in fearful union . . .' Iconicity blurs the boundary between illusionistic and experiential space. By no coincidence, in San Francisco and then New York Still relished a confined studio set-up and the paintings themselves pull us up short into a kind of reactive self-awareness. With much cut by the

138

frame, more seems to be going on beyond it, just as the broken edgings feel animistic – thus their uncanny grip: 'the best works are often those with the fewest and simplest elements . . . until you look at them a little more, and things start to happen' (Still).

Although no mutual influence existed between Still and Guston they shared the capacity to turn traumatic content into an intensifying and therefore positive aesthetic experience. Having gone from Iowa City to a teaching post in St Louis, Guston renewed his study of Beckmann and Picasso in a fashion that led away from *If This Be Not I* (1945) to the much flatter if equally beguiled allegory of *Night Children* (1946) and next the cut-out stylization of *Performers* and *Porch II* (both 1947). In the meantime he was struck by the newsreels of rag-doll Holocaust corpses. With that knowledge *Porch II* weaves a   105 congested disquiet where the carnival figures with their musical instruments become victims to the pressure of the picture plane (on which a shoe sole is brutally imprinted at bottom left) and an armature of wooden struts and inert planes. Whether or not Guston knew it, he had also approximated the same stiff gesturing and forlorn symbols for the human predicament that Ben Shahn, Stephen Greene and other allegorical 'realists' were using. A desire to strike away from this well-worn formula is confirmed in *The Tormentors* (1947–48) and its   106, 107

104 Clyfford Still *1948-E*

study. Their components remain Guston's old props: trumpet, architectural outlines, a Klansman's arm and the dotted hobnail crescent of a heel that calls to mind Orwell's dire prophecy of the future as a boot stamping on a human face for ever. This is the nightmarish jumble of people, things and perceptual shifts with which the novelist John Hawkes would portray postwar disorientation in *The Cannibal* (1949). But whereas the pathos of *Porch II* was obvious, here it lingers in a tremulous scrawny touch that Guston would make his own, the attrition of solids to vestiges and a dying light.

118   With a leave of absence from Washington University in 1947 Guston began *Review* (1948–50) in Woodstock, New York State, before his Prix de Rome year in Italy and finished it upon return. The darkness has gathered into an upper field that oppresses a red region below embedded with fragile, shadowed memories of an earlier vocabulary. An involved facture, recalling his first-hand contact with the oils of the Venetian school in 1948, leaves us to decipher the many traces that resist the swell of red and penumbral browns. Again we are drawn into a perceptual act that is inevitably prolonged or fraught and according to Dore Ashton the artist would speak of 'reading' the language of paint.

140

106 Philip Guston *The Tormentors* 1947–48

107 Philip Guston, study for *The Tormentors* 1947

Perhaps the most closely reasoned of any shift away from overt figuration took place as Rothko, in his own words of 1947, 'pulverized the familiar identity of things' to unite the mid-1940s hieratic beings with a primal haze or aether that together would slowly expand into chromatic zones. Later he told Seitz, 'It was not that the figure had been removed, not that the figures had been swept away, but the symbols for the figures, and in turn the shapes in the later canvases were substitutes for the figures. . . . These new shapes say . . . what the symbols said.'

At first Rothko toyed with complete dissolution in, for example, *Number 18* where, despite its residual schema for a square upright torso and oblong head, everything appears to pulsate; this was succeeded by an emergent clarity that he connected in a 1949 *Tiger's Eye* statement with 'the elimination of all obstacles between the painter and the idea and between the idea and the observer'. Like Still, Guston and Newman, he envisaged the vehicle for this unmediated experience to be a spatial field able to envelop the spectator. His special discovery was a format invested at once with powers of self-denial (so that we absorb the 'breathing' luminosity) and memories of those rectilinear elements that had brought ominous constraint to the compositions since the 1930s (so the sensuousness is tense). In the 1948–49 paintings including the *Multiform* series dilute oil washes soak into the canvas even as they form rectangles echoing the frame in a Mondrianesque fashion. Nor is Rothko likely to have missed the 1948 Bonnard retrospective at MoMA and its display of disembodied, shimmering

108 Mark Rothko
Untitled 1948

109 Mark Rothko
Number 22 c. 1949

radiance. At the middle of *Number 22* (*c.* 1949) three gouged lines move to a nexus, the last remnants of the wiry organisms entombed within the surrounding strata during his former biomorphic phase. Otherwise every incidental has been absorbed by the huge veils of red and gold, frontal yet nuanced, silent but so sheer as to fill the mind.

Behind the search for intensity that reached its climax in colour as field ran the years when some intellectuals saw American society as foreclosed. Either, in their estimate, historical forces were massing into the new technocratic brand of extremism personified by the General Cummings character ('You can consider the army a preview of the future') in Norman Mailer's *The Naked and the Dead* (1948); or people had become the unfeeling conformists censured in the sociologist David Riesman's *The Lonely Crowd* (1950); or culture itself

was being bankrupted by the rise of the mass media (1948 saw the first
television faking of an event), consumerism, advertising, suburbia, and the pervasive propagandism of the Truman era. Thus the choices looked stark: alienated despair, praise for the all-American way of life (as evinced by most former *Partisan Review* 'radicals') or the oppositional stance taken by Still, Rothko and Newman. This was when their embattled self-images matured into a polemical frame of mind that gave painting the status of a moral critique. It had the extremism – compelling and even absurd – of a time when open political activity was dangerous and dissent spelled ostracism. Henceforth Still for example denounced American materialism and in a July 1950 letter he linked the 'magnitude' and 'intensity' of Newman's colour to a total rejection of contemporary culture and those behind it. Freed of a false sense of security, community and of the plastic bank-book, wrote Rothko in his 'The Romantics Were Prompted' essay (1947–48), 'transcendental experiences become possible'. Alienation had to be resisted or else it would prompt the escapism of the Romantics and their latter-day heirs. Here Newman's contribution came to the fore.

70   If *The Death of Euclid* (1947), *The Command* (1946), *Euclidean Abyss* (1946–47) and *Genetic Moment* (1947) are understood alongside Newman's written theorizing they reveal a strategy to dramatize the apocalyptic situation after the Holocaust and Hiroshima so that out of chaos would rise an abstract image that in 'The Sublime is Now' (1948) he called 'real and concrete' and therefore the opposite of alienation. Strange shafts slice through the bleakness of those pictures: quite untouched, they resemble absolutes amid chaotic gulfs. Underlying such polarities lay the rather Germanic cast of his thought with its dialectic shaping the essays then that contrast 'man' and 'nature', 'order' against 'terror', 'beauty' versus 'sublimity'. An important source was the German art historian Wilhelm Worringer's claims that abstraction, far from being empty and unreal, embodied acute emotions in the face of terrible circumstances. A friendly world, wrote Worringer, led instead to empathy and hence the 'realism' that Newman in turn regarded as bogus. In 1947–48 the verticals altered as Newman 'became involved with light' and in several brush and ink drawings they become radiant entities that command the gloom. Giacometti's sculptures at the Pierre Matisse Gallery in February 1948 also impressed him with their ultra-thin figures that still defied the surrounding emptiness. On 29 January however, he had already put a line of masking tape down the centre of a dark cadmium red field,

overpainted it with a glowing orange–red and pondered the result for almost a year. It was at once an end and a beginning.

Until *Onement I* Newman's ideas had been grand, their realization often meagre. Now the image and the symbol of genesis were seamlessly knit. Though physically small, this unity renders the canvas grand in scale and the same applies to the forthrightness that Still and Rothko reached. At vital points in the course of Western art clarity or directness have been idealized. One thinks of the austerity of the early Renaissance, David's spartan *Oath of the Horatii* (1784) and Mondrian defying a murderous present when he chose to purify his idiom at the height of the First World War. Each call to order had moral implications and this was no exception. For with even Henry Wallace's moderate Progressive Party defeated in 1948 in a campaign of anti-Communist hysteria and smears, civil liberties everywhere attacked, the defeat of labour in the 1945–46 strikes followed by severe counter-measures, modern art denounced from the floor of Congress and writers returning to myth, formalism or proclaiming the death of the hero, the noumenal impact of colour vitalizing space represented something singular and beyond assailment. This is why Still could say in a now lost statement for his 1950 show, 'Through them [the paintings] I breathe again' and Rothko, 'It is really a matter of ending this silence and solitude, of breathing and stretching one's arms again' ('The Romantics . . .'). Against the perceived spiritual prison of postwar history these metaphors of resurrection – verbal and imagistic – make sense.

That we can surmount time and apprehend things absolutely are of course illusions but nevertheless potent, even therapeutic ones, especially when the times appear out of joint, life stymied and culture debased. Scale and colour engineer those illusions. Both can be interiorized and hence galvanize us, as Braque noted with his comment that colour 'either absorbs or is absorbed'. Size is an objective measurement, scale involves the humanly subjective experience of measure. The openness of *Onement I* (symmetrical and upright like ourselves) makes it elemental, a head-on meeting between vision and redness. Newman paraphrased that fixity when he said, 'The self, terrible and constant, is for me the subject-matter of painting.' In 1945 he wrote about exploring the whole 'octave' of a hue and the 'zip' of *Onement I* sounds the highest note of a scale given by the field's pedal point. At a stroke the previous break between vertical and void was converted into a wholeness, a continuum ('instead of working with the remnants of space, I work with the whole space'). From here onwards the paintings await our completion as we become the human focus in a rapport with radiance, darkness or varieties of balance. The compositions locate us; so long as the moment lasts the sense of self prevails. Why else should there have been an exact coincidence between this extraordinary role that absolute chroma conferred on the observer, the artists' conviction that states of being were at stake and an America where the free individual was equated with publicly censured 'subversives' who included Einstein, Oppenheimer and Chaplin? When Newman remarked (as quoted in Chapter 5) that his paintings spelt the end of state capitalism and totalitarianism he maintained that their 'open world' denoted the possibility of 'an open society'.

By the turn of the decade Still, Rothko and Newman went beyond easel dimensions to formats that passed from a discrete rectangle hung on the wall into a phenomenon less dwarfing than a true mural but vast enough to offer a personal challenge of a kind reflecting the current revival of interest in the concept of the sublime. Originally codified by the first- or second-century AD Greek philosopher Longinus who related it to the expression of a grandeur of ideas, the sublime only returned as a full-blown aesthetic with the rise of Romanticism when Edmund Burke and Immanuel Kant defined it as the mind's experience of being exalted by enormity, vacuity, darkness, solitude, silence and infinity. Yet the mere spectacular aspect, already thoroughly treated by nineteenth-century American landscape painters, held no real appeal now. Burke's sensationalism, joked Newman, was a bit 'Surrealist'. Rather, the sublime meant another strategy towards the intensification of human experience especially since it was already a truism – witness the *New Yorker* cartoon and the rise during the late 1940s of supermarkets, synthetics, kitsch and what Herbert Marcuse would later dub 'one-dimensional' man – that Americans had never been so removed from authenticity. Engulfing and inescapable, the big picture would enhance the self. Rothko even denied Romantic flamboyance: 'I realize that historically the function of painting large pictures is painting something very grandiose and pompous. The reason I paint them, however – I think it applies to other painters I know – is precisely because I want to be very intimate and human' (1951). Or, according to Still in December 1949, his paintings placed the viewer before them 'on his own'. What did these aspirations contravene if not that slide into dehumanization that bedevilled America after 1945 when it rapidly became the world's greatest consumer economy? By 1951 Ernst Haas could photograph a

110 Barnett Newman *Cathedra* 1951, installation view, 1958

111 Gardner Rea, 'One nice thing about TV . . .' *New Yorker* cartoon, 1951

"One nice thing about television, you don't have to pick out where to look."

drive-in church peopled by cars, institutionalized religion had degenerated into cant, the McCarthyite witch hunt was nearing a peak and the Korean debacle threatened. Without this perspective on the year when Newman finished *Vir Heroicus Sublimis* we miss the full import of the title, meaning roughly 'man, heroic and sublime', and its form.

147

Instantly the 140 or so square feet of redness that is *Vir Heroicus Sublimis* locks the beholder into his or her act of communion. Who cannot apprehend redness yet who can define it? Whether it is this
120   blaze, the preternatural ultramarine of *Cathedra* (1951), the all-black *Abraham* (1949) or the all-white *The Voice* and *The Name* (both 1950), each hue is declared with a sweep that humbles description. Here the 'zips' function by acting as our guides to the potentially inchoate field as they focus, measure and stabilize the gaze. A comparison with Ad Reinhardt is elucidating. During the 1940s his geometric planes dissolved into all-over calligraphy but then in a cyclical change he was

148

beguiled (most probably by Newman, Rothko and Still) into employing more unified fields of colour that give off a steady glow. But these large, near-monochrome compositions remain classically aloof, their equipoise static, whereas Newman's 'zips' summon a dynamic response. If solitary the latter are analogous to sound in a silence which by its very isolation seems meant for us alone and so begins a dialogue. This factor underpins Newman's references to sound or speech in such titles as *Concord*, *The Promise* and *Outcry*. When augmented to the array that leaves no stretch of *Vir Heroicus Sublimis* without its pulse of light or shade (each of the five verticals is of a different value), then it is up to us in the perceptual act which is almost flooded by redness to unite those stanchion presences that endure as well. Facing the perfect square framed by the two innermost 'zips', yet aware of their echoes that resound to the outer margins, ours is the true 'vital center' before *Vir Heroicus Sublimis*. 112 125

Nothing has denatured Abstract Expressionism more than the Greenbergian view which isolates its chromatic expanses in a tradition of increasingly flat Modernist painting supposed to have run from Impressionism to Post-Painterly Abstraction in the 1960s. Certainly Rothko for one knew such prototypes through his love for Matisse (to whom he dedicated a 1954 canvas) and its continuation in the lyrical art of his friend Milton Avery. But, again, he was touched by Fra Angelico, Rembrandt, Turner, and stressed (alongside Still, Guston and Newman) how colour offered a means not an end, consequently calling his rectangles 'things' – an odd word, unless understood as his way of emphasizing that they were still what he had once named 'actors' rather than insubstantial patterns. Fields are furthermore ultimate states of space and space tells of the human condition.

Being and field have an intertwined history. The more extreme the expanse, the closer it skirts both emptiness and immanence. Intimations of loneliness or human singularity seem implicit in extensity itself, a paradox which had not been lost on the Romantics. To cite only a few examples: certain sparse landscapes by Caspar David Friedrich, Goya's unique *Dog buried in Sand* (1820–23) and even the 'Prelude' to Wagner's *Das Rheingold* (1869) all explore primordially monolithic structures that are at once voids yet pregnant with signs of life. Dostoyevsky's notebooks for *The Idiot* (1868–69) mention a 'field of action' as a backdrop for the main protagonist and Mallarmé's poetry had eulogized blankness. Laden with similar connotations, the field of space returned to serve the strain of existential angst in America that drifted on from the Depression to wartime and after. 113

115, 116
114 Stark voids or fields of minute detail trap and alienate the human presence in memorable figurative paintings by Ben Shahn and Andrew Wyeth as well as in the lesser-known work of Perlin, Robert Vickrey and the photographer Harry Callahan who was a friend of Siskind. Theodore Roethke's poems such as 'Unfold! Unfold!' (1951) make the field a psychological continuum and by the time Hitchcock set Cary Grant adrift in the blank yet tense Midwest expanses of the crop-dusting scene of *North By Northwest* (1959) the paradox of 'empty' space fomenting human drama was virtually a cliché.

Avant-gardism to the Abstract Expressionists meant that further reach where the field kept its established symbolism but encompassed more than orthodox realism could. Instead of depicting figure against field they meant to draw the onlooker into the former's standpoint. Newman pinned a note on the wall at his 1950 Betty Parsons show counselling the viewer to stand close so that erstwhile self-sufficient images modulate into chromatic light. When he eschews 'zips' altogether the fields themselves are structured to make us the pivot of crisis. In the very tall pictures *Day Before One* (1951), *Day One* (1951–

114 Andrew Wyeth *Winter* 1946

115 Ben Shahn *Pacific Landscape* 1945

116 Ben Shahn *Handball* 1939

52), *Prometheus Bound* (1952) and *Primordial Light* (1954) perception is stretched to a limit as one vast wall of hue seemingly cloaks another that manages, barely, to burst loose at its edge. The force of the paintings is in the eye's struggle to reconcile inertia and a precisely focused edge or break. A similar charge attaches itself to the rifts that disturb Still's monoliths and the edgings around Rothko's rectangles. Playing upon maxima and minima, stasis and revelatory incident, such technique tests our faculties at first hand and so confounds reproduction. As Newman stated, 'They are specific, and separate embodiments of feeling, to be experienced, each picture for itself' (1950). Saturation embodied emotional force. Once Rothko confided that his colours were compressed like gases to explosion-point and Still wrote to Newman in 1950 about colour that could 'burn' its way through a man's guts. Still's own textures were intended to 'bite' using powder pigments, glazes, slashes and dry weals scraped from the palette. The astringency finishes what the petrified figures of the 1930s had begun. Any illusion is 'killed' (again his word) by the layering that

117 Aaron Siskind
Chicago 1947–48

118 Philip Guston
Review 1948–50

remains terribly immediate, all foreground, their crudeness a deliber-
ate affront to that habit of processing everything which Still thought
had emasculated postwar Americans who wanted, in the topical
syntax of his metaphors, 'a sedative . . . not a bull in the field, but a
Howard Johnson hamburger'.

Parallelism rather than influence accounts for Siskind's work
appearing to recapitulate Still's. Although the latter exhibited at Betty
Parsons in 1947, 1950 and 1951 Siskind had independently eliminated
depth and even forecasted the future in 1945 when he envisaged an
'unyielding space' where 'there is only the drama of objects, and you,
watching.' After 1947 he focused ever more minutely upon decayed
and paint-smeared walls whose facades, dense with graphic traces, 117
apparently make darkness visible. Our task is again to delve the surface
as though it were an adversary for signs of intent. Admittedly,
comparable traumas are evident in the muteness that often froze
people in contemporary realist painting and the literature of
alienation. But their voids and palimpsests remain backdrops whereas
the Abstract Expressionist field provokes a dialectic, sometimes by
means of disjointed signification. Before Still's *Painting 1952*, caught 119
between the gigantic charred abyss (the field), an anchor of slate grey
(the cornerstone motif at the bottom right) and a razor-edge lifeline

119 Clyfford Still *Painting 1952*

(the off-centre white vertical) our attention encounters a crossroads. In recoil from the black barrier the onlooker fastens upon glimmers of light and stability. If cartoons might satirize apathy and serious realists portray alienation, this is catharsis.

The tensions of engagement also concerned Rothko who said, 'a painting lives by companionship, expanding and quickening in the eyes of the observer' (1947), as if, in other words, it subtly tested human sentience. The famous stacked rectangles of colour that were finalized by 1950 and infinitely varied thereafter consummated his call seven years before for 'the simple expression of the complex thought'.

One of Rothko's first loves was the theatre and his mature format hints, like a proscenium, that events are to happen. Symmetrical, regular and open, it also entrances. So does a technique which employs the devices of illusionist rendering: finely gradated values, scumbles and a palette either warm or saturated enough to emanate sensuality.

154

Yet the presentation is deceptive since the fields, being effaced, are enigmas. Rothko once thought that Wyeth was about 'the pursuit of strangeness' and admired de Chirico, Dali and especially Hopper, all alike fascinated by mysteriously vacant but luminous space. Abstraction, however, allowed him further complexities. Colours gain a mercurial life and, as in the Wallace Stevens poetry that he liked to discuss, untoward permutations suggest the metaphysical. The lower zone of *Untitled 1954*, for instance, vacillates between a lilac veneer, a   127
deeper reddish glow and a violet that glimmers far below while, somehow, the ensemble still hovers in unison. Akin to a view out of a glass window, depth appears to well up through flatness and, interestingly, psychological tests confirm that diffuse edges convey volume to otherwise flat planes. Guston's early 1950s oils were even more keyed to this potential in a pervasive spreading haze. In *Red Painting* (1950) and *White Painting* (1951) it permeates the end traces of figuration, a process one suspects was stimulated by a spell in southern Europe's light (the drawings from Ischia in 1949 have a new delicacy) and by his composer friends Morton Feldman and John Cage who were exploring ethereal sounds and their relation to silence. *Painting*   126
1952 connects tinted strands into a tapestry that dissolves back to a field nearer the edges. As the thicker marks are vestiges of past forms, so the mistiness implies time's passage and in 1959 Guston called painting a 'tug of war . . . between the moment and the pull of memory'. If even these interweavings were stilled to tremors, their structure opened out and the tones intensified, we should be closer to the archetypal 1950s Rothko. Neither abstract landscapes (despite the elemental divisions), nor figures (despite the upright organization and haloes), Rothko avowed in a 1958 lecture that they were 'facades'. And facades both reveal and conceal. Never has that hypnotic irony been better described than by Nietzsche, unwittingly, in *The Birth of Tragedy* (1872), a book Rothko knew well:

We looked at the drama . . . whose most profound meaning we almost thought we could guess and that we wished to draw away like a curtain in order to behold the primordial image behind it. The brightest clarity of the image did not suffice us, for this seemed to wish just as much to reveal something as to conceal it. Its revelation, being like a parable, seemed to summon us to tear the veil and to uncover the mysterious background; but simultaneously this all-illuminated, total visibility cast a spell over the eyes and prevented them from penetrating deeper.

With smooth unbroken surfaces everywhere the quintessence of impersonality in postwar America, from the Eames chair to the

120 Barnett Newman *Cathedra* 1951

Miesian office, Rothko seems to go quietly against the grain in paintings that imbue them with doubt and awe. In comparison, Newman's address the individual like a clarion and his titles range from imperatives (*Be*) to singular states (*Onement*), moments (*Day One*) and choices (*The Way*), or assert the unique spot to be (*Cathedra*, a locus, literally a throne, of great power) and affirm the heroic (*Adam*, *Vir Heroicus Sublimis*). To understand the implications we must recall not just Newman's Jewish humanism but also how the concept of the heroic individual was criticized by 'liberals' like Lionel Trilling then (and had vanished from realist painting) together with social mores, media, novels, films and an environmental ambience itself (the blandly uniform, sprawling suburbia) which lauded the virtues of a person *not* standing out until the sociologist William Whyte in *The Organization Man* (1956) wrote that the nation's ethic was to believe that 'of himself, [man] is isolated, meaningless.' Yet Newman's *The Wild* (1950), Smith's *The Hero* (1951–52) and de Kooning's *Woman I* (1950–52) reaffirm the outstanding fact of humanness on a scale that stretches from the sublime to the absurd.

The Wild presents a crimson shaft on a dark ground narrow enough to be breathtaking – as though one's presence were suddenly surrounded by infinity. Rising upright and apart, the distinctness of the onlooker is returned and its sculptural counterpart is Smith's *The Hero* which shares the same culturally loaded theme of the vertical

156

entity commanding space. Though Jacques Lipchitz's malign columnar *Figure* of 1926–30 advised it, *The Hero* looks freed from Smith's
surreal or aggressive erotic neuroses of the 1940s to an extent that other
American sculptors who are sometimes designated 'Abstract Expressionists' had not attained. Greenberg's evaluation of Seymour Lipton,
Roszak, Richard Lippold, Ferber *et alia* remains a killing analysis of
why Smith's clipped and facient style belongs to the movement and
theirs in the end do not: 'the most conspicuous result of the diffusion of

123

122 Barnett Newman *The Wild* 1950, installation
view with *Here I* at left

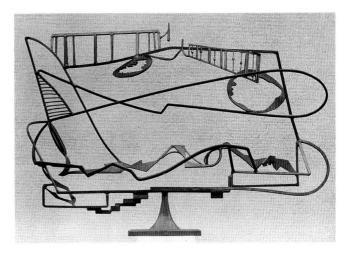

123 David Smith *The Hero* 1951–52

124 David Smith *Hudson River Landscape* 1951

the use of the welding torch . . . has turned out to be garden statuary, oversized objets d'art and monstrous costume jewelry' (*David Smith*, 1956). The stature of *The Hero*, like that of *The Wild*, affirms rather than threatens, the two points that represent breasts imply psychic unity between the male and female principles since Smith named it a self-portrait, and the steel's industrial rigour (brazened by red lead paint) is met with the vacancy within the rectangular body. This presents the *tabula rasa* open to the future and in superb complementary horizontal pieces such as *Star Cage* (1950), *Australia* and *Hudson River Landscape* (both 1951), the latter based partly on aerial photographs and train journeys through upstate New York, Smith exalted the transcendence of boundaries between space and time. By assimilating Pollock's 1947–50 idiom these sculptures approach fields wherein linear contours and intervals, sky and earth motifs, the pedestal and the outspread vectors flow together with an ease that expresses the multiplicity of being. In notes for an article of 1951 Smith added: 'Sculpture is as free as the mind; as complex as life . . .'

Only a pictorial mode that accommodated complexity satisfied de Kooning after *Excavation* left for the Venice Biennale in 1950. Either he could progress into utter abstractness or renew the figures that had made a comeback in the late 1940s. Instead he did both. *Woman I* started with felt 'reality' as a mouth ('the smile was something to hang onto') from a magazine advertisement stuck upon the painting.

125 *top* Ad Reinhardt *Painting 1950*

126 Philip Guston *Painting 1952*

127 Mark Rothko *Untitled* 1954

This was a kaleidoscope of disjointed limbs and indications of an interior. After two years of continual revision it reached a decisive incompleteness with the human element regenerated upon a ground of furious entropy harking back to *Excavation* and representative of the urban flux without rest or form which de Kooning called a 'no-environment'. Shortly before, the predatory Gloria Swanson had transfixed American cinema screens at the end of Billy Wilder's *Sunset Boulevard* (1950) and *Woman I* rises to command her frame with the same preposterous iconicity. She is Pater's Mona Lisa, half vampire, half secular madonna, for the Broadway neon. In a patriarchal society she furthermore lampooned gender stereotypes from the All-American Mom to the career-girl vixen which the feminist Betty Friedan would later unveil as adjuncts of the era's 'feminine mystique'. If the mid-1940s women had been sadly beleaguered, de Kooning singled out the 'hilariousness' of the new series of which six were shown at the Sidney Janis Gallery in 1953. This comic–heroic vitality informs the signification of *Woman I* which lets two variant messages coexist: the frontally emphatic gaze, grin, breasts and bodily mass ('flesh', the artist said, 'was the reason why oil paint was invented') defy surroundings which are blurred as when glimpsed for a split second. *Excavation* churned life under the pictorial field; the *Women* surge out of it.

CHAPTER SEVEN

The Later Work

The 1950s involved a mixture of impasse, retrenchment and fresh departures. Those who formulated radical styles soonest tended to examine where they could go next, aware of the dangers of becoming prisoners of their own originality. With their masterpieces of the late 1940s and early 1950s Pollock, de Kooning, Still, Rothko, Newman, Guston, Smith and Siskind belong in this category. Overall a profile emerged that differentiates the later work – bearing in mind the timespan of the individual careers. It included a return to figuration and sometimes more imposingly 'public' or rhetorical styles; works in series; dissimilar idioms juxtaposed in the same image; and projects of an environmental scope. The last, whether in the form of Rothko's three late mural series or the artists' preference that their opus should be seen at once *in toto* yet by itself, tied in with a longstanding aim to control the observer's experience. 148

Inadequate documentation means that no exact order of precedence within the whole movement is ever likely to suffice. But a case exists for locating the first generation on a scale that falls away from the vanguard above. Neither Motherwell nor Kline were quite sure of their paths until each discovered a formula – the stark elements of *At Five in the Afternoon* and the massive black and white brushmarks that Kline finally chose in 1949–50 – which felt abstract but evocative enough to yield numerous future variations. Whereas others concentrated their styles to an essence, these resolutions seem different, closer indeed to breakthroughs than consummations and so, ironically, open to extension. 82

The germ of *At Five in the Afternoon* was a 1948 'illumination' by Motherwell to a Rosenberg poem. This pen and ink sketch began as an automatist doodle which he then restructured towards the future *Elegy* format of ovoids against verticals. The will to forego figuration and also its subsequent growth into the larger *Granada* (1949) and the really big 1950s versions has a calculated quality. Similarly Kline's maturation as late as 1950 (the date of his first one-man show at the Egan Gallery) was predicated on Tomlin, Pollock and de Kooning. 132

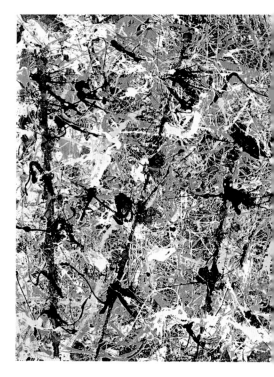

129 Jackson Pollock *Blue Poles*
1952

130 Jackson Pollock *Portrait and a Dream* 1953

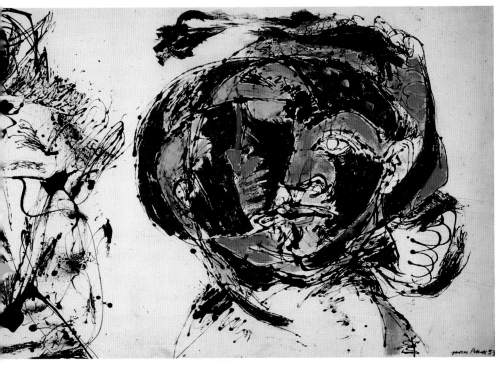

It was the paradigm of these artists that bolstered his command of calligraphic gesture; the last even gave him a better insight into scale in 1948 or 1949 by enlarging some of his recent ink drawings with a Bell-Opticon projector. Most belatedly of all, Gottlieb continued the 'Pictographs' until 1952 when the more painterly meshwork 'Grids' and the 'Imaginary Landscapes' such as *Frozen Sounds II* (1952) simplified his pictographic symbols into discs and flat emblems levitated above turbulent horizons. These made way for the 'Bursts' in 1957 where circular forms (often with slight haloes) are counterpoised against gestural eruptions beneath. At his death in 1974 Gottlieb was still engaged upon them.

131

The merits and weakness inherent in the later careers of Kline, Motherwell and especially Gottlieb exemplify a movement at the point when it had become ripe enough to codify. Symbolism is looked after by a syntax of opposites: of black against white, or 'active' presences cleaving 'neutral' space. There is a technical virtuosity rather than inspiration in the high impasto that answers passages of thin

squeegee-applied paint in the 'Bursts'. Excitement stays, literally and metaphorically, near the surfaces which impress but do not draw the viewer psychologically inwards, since – and this is the surest symptom of decline – they revert to a conventional space where shapes stand upon a background. Perhaps seeing these pitfalls, Motherwell diversified himself the most. His 'Open' canvases (1967 onwards) unite the wall–window imagery harking back to *The Little Spanish Prison* with lucent colour fields and in large collages from the 1970s an unmistakably Abstract Expressionist vivacity invigorates many passing glances to European culture, including the conventions of Cubism itself. Cosmopolitanism informs the *Elegies* as well, numbering over one hundred with minor and destroyed versions counted. They encompass history as private trauma in Motherwell's overall commemoration of the Spanish Civil War as 'a terrible death . . . that should not be forgot'; psychological drives in the brutal phallic lunges of *No. 34*; the architectonic design of *No. 54* that recalls his admiration for a certain photograph of a Greek temple at dusk; and the purely *ad*

132

133 Willem de Kooning *Door to the River* 1960

134 Franz Kline *Mahoning* 1956

hoc improvisation of *The Figure 4 on an Elegy* (1960). Motherwell always remained an outstanding technician, adept at raising colour to a philosophical pitch.

So idiosyncratic a style as Kline's instead held him in thrall and, apart from returning to a full palette in the later 1950s, it never altered a great deal before his premature death with a rheumatic heart in 1962. Yet he was the complete master of a métier that alongside de Kooning's 133 turned 'gesturalism' from a concept into a look that could be adopted by another generation, secondary either in years or invention and confusingly also called 'The New York School', whose more notable members included Jack Tworkov, Joan Mitchell, and Alfred Leslie. Compared to their more lyrical, decorative or simply dull handling which Greenberg dubbed 'the 10th St Touch', Kline's has the assurance which distinguishes founders from acolytes.

Fortunately Kline pushed a restricted vocabulary to its utmost. Great bands and wedges of black jostled by the white (and not merely 134 on top of it) form grids, sometimes enlivened with loops or arcs, which defy the borders to thrust outwards. He named this stirring instability 'the awkwardness of "not balance"' and, again, it was rehearsed with some care in the abundant sketches on telephone directory pages which chart his search for motifs that would unite the impromptu and the monolithic. In the open square of *Wotan* (1950) all is purged to a few gargantuan slashes often likened to Oriental calligraphy, even though Kline denied the link. At another extreme, evident from around the time of *Siegfried* (1958) and after, his erstwhile sharp tonal contrasts coalesce into stormy greys. Overt or implicit, the grid structure connotes the urban and mechanistic energies Kline relished in the industrialism of his native Pennsylvania coal country and of course in Manhattan itself, where melodramatic silhouettes prevail and diagonals within a right-angled universe suggest sudden lurches against the pattern. Working under strong lights with housepainter's brushes and enamels, frequently at night, made for a surface which in conjunction with the tiny splatters and scrapings around the blacks radiates an explosive velocity. Like Kline's persona, the mode is one of Yankee toughness alongside titles which further encourage a reading of the images as metaphors for concrete 134 experience with their place names (*Scranton* and *Mahoning* are in Pennsylvania), enthusiasms (*Siegfried* and others tell of a passion for Wagner) and things (*Cardinal* and *Chief* had been coal-country locomotive names) that constitute a personal inventory. A critique of the strident late works incorporating greens, flames and saturated blue must lie in the eloquence Kline had extracted from monochrome.

Those without a place in the Abstract Expressionist front ranks, because their contributions were either curtailed, derivative or somehow became ingrown, warrant only brief mention here. Tomlin comes under the first category due to his death in 1953, though one still doubts whether by then he had done more than bond calligraphic signs from the 1940s onto a Cubist infrastructure. His was a quiet temperament, anyway, and given to cool harmonies whose all-over 64 yet self-contained meanderings suggest the 'classical' Pollock as viewed by a careful draughtsman who probably studied Chinese and Sanskrit scripts.

Despite chronological membership of the first generation James Brooks, Esteban Vicente and Conrad Marca-Relli, the last a skilful exponent since 1953 of collage mixed with oils on canvas, all mark the point where once-personal styles shade into traits – fluent, agitated or exposed linear rhythms and intercalated colour zones – shuffled about

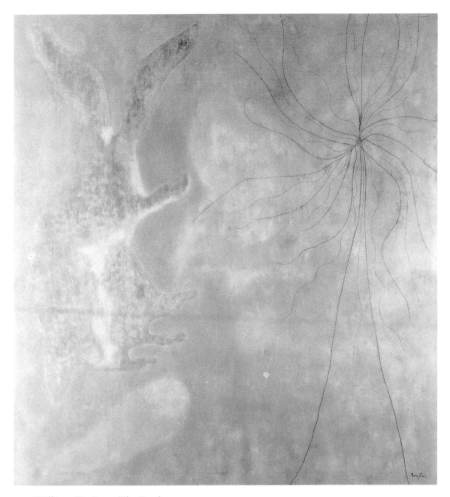

135 William Baziotes *The Pond* 1955

as in some pastiche. Similar reservations apply to much 1950s 'New York School' painting. Reminders of the adage about the second rate creating a period style permeate this entire chapter and the label 'Abstract Impressionism' coined for the hazy mirages of Milton Resnick purveys an apt ersatz flavour. The destinies of Stamos, Baziotes and Pousette-Dart pose a trickier problem. Each had kept abreast with the mythic, ideographic and biomorphic trends of the 1940s but contributed less over the next decade when Baziotes returned to meticulously limned amoeboid creatures that glide

135

through steamy gulfs whose tones, as Still thoughtfully said in 1970, plumb 'minor chords'. As with Stamos in general and Pousette-Dart after what were impressive incandescent totems in *Blood Wedding* (1950), lapidary effects meant to evoke the cosmic betray a lack of impetus, of craftsmanship hiding foreclosed imaginations. This is a classic malady in those distanced from an evolving art scene and few suffered it more than Hofmann during his first postwar decade.

Advanced in years but still running art schools in New York and Provincetown, Hofmann, as late as *Orchestral Dominance in Green* (1954), foundered in an aesthetic hinterland where thick surfaces and livid colours were supposed to burst the shackles of a faceted armature out of 1911–12 'analytical' Cubism. Nor had his competing idioms so resembled someone wandering in a time warp than when he jumped from the quasi-geometric still-life *Magenta and Blue* (1950) to the biomorph in *Flight* (1952) taken from Picasso's 1929 *Woman by the Sea*. Then, unexpectedly, all was transformed. In his late seventies Hofmann found the integrity that had eluded him and embarked on his 'signature' paintings where dazzling rectangular slabs, sculpted by the knife with hard edges, dilate through thinner atmospheric expanses. Though the material was long dormant in his theories about extracting planar tensions from reality, a suspicion arises that this final burst was lit by an outside spark: having fallen behind those he had formerly inspired, Hofmann now switched places again. His Indian summer was a review of Abstract Expressionist mannerisms by a cerebral yet outgoing sensibility quite alien to its spirit. 'Action' painting is recast as carefully reckless brushwork while the rich concentrated tones mirror Rothko, Newman and Still (especially his knack of electrifying a colour with smaller grace notes). Beside theirs, his remain easel pictures that frame a hierarchy of elements in equilibrium and are closer to the School of Paris abstraction done by, say, de Staël, Riopelle and Soulages; except that behind Hofmann's voluptuous pictorial cadences one notices a pairing of lusty exuberance and craft somewhat familiar in old painters (think of Titian and Picasso).

But what about the other major figures? As the 1950s continued, contradictions disturbed them. Full acclaim came slowly, held its own dangers and was not synonymous with quick financial reward. Not until well into the decade did sales appreciate after *Fortune* magazine in 1955 pinpointed them as potential 'growth stocks' and Pollock's death added a mystique and the historical closure necessary to attract not just the modestly or newly affluent (so far almost the sole collectors) but

136 Hans Hofmann *Memoria in Aeternum* 1962

the very rich who had hitherto favoured European artworks. A Pollock sold for $30,000 in 1958 and thereafter prices rose. Yet the differential between market profits and the artists' incomes was considerable or at worst eroded only posthumously. Private tensions dated from the first half of the 1950s when Pollock, Rothko and de Kooning, malcontent with Betty Parsons, abandoned her gallery for Sidney Janis's. Inter-personal rapport also deteriorated and the bitterness that arose amongst Still, Newman, Rothko and Reinhardt (and later involved Motherwell) never entirely went. It was of the type that develops between kindred souls. They were also ill at ease with success. Even worse, Cold War supporters numbering the Rockefeller family and the CIA itself helped promote Abstract Expressionism at home and abroad via such agencies as MoMA, which mounted a sequence of exhibitions whose summit was 'The New American Painting' that toured eight European countries in 1958–59. Consequently the movement became enshrined as America's aesthetic ambassador to the world and a symbol of its superior freedoms. Whether all this reflected a conspiracy or the coincidence of innovative art with a nation at the zenith of imperial power appears less consequential than that the artists never engineered it. Their 'Americanness' remains harder to assess. Endemic myths about the nation's vigour had been strong influences upon their generation, reborn in Still's polemics against the moribund Old World, in Newman's texts of the 1940s where America is linked to primal energies and throughout their love–hate relations with European painting and sculpture itself. However, apologists began insidiously to harden those features into more of a mask during the Cold War. From Rosenberg's 'The American Action Painters' through Greenberg's knowingly titled '"American-Type" Painting' to Sandler's 'The Triumph of American Painting' (which appeared in 1970 when the international status of America in the Vietnam era was again at issue) there runs the same faint chauvinism. In less careful hands it produced stereotypes cast in the American grain.

So it is fitting to see beneath otherwise separate later events a wish to outrun clichés and to break moulds. This had already speeded de Kooning's notable volte-face in the *Women*. Smith's sheer fecundity, ever expanding after better finances in the 1950s meant more materials, reflected his disdain for categorization in favour of a process or, as he put it, a 'work stream' flowing from sculpture to graphics and paintings. In his old age Newman diversified into the sculptures that number *Here II* and *III* (1965/66), *Broken Obelisk* (1963–67), the politicized barbed wire *Lace Curtain for Mayor Daley* (1968), designs for a synagogue (1963) and lithography. The cyclical pattern of Siskind's maturity, when experiments like the divers snapped in mid-air of *Pleasures and Terrors of Levitation* (1953–61) alternate with trips to Mexico, Rome, Hawaii and South America, represents another way of avoiding the pitfalls inherent in a linear evolution which had engendered the unique excitement of much that was created after the War by a

logic that went to the limits of his starkest wall images, *The Wild*, and
Pollock's dripped paintings. But brinksmanship could not last for
ever.

'I've had a period of drawing on canvas in black – with some of my
early images coming thru – think the non-objectivists will find them
disturbing – and the kids who think it simple to splash a Pollock out.'
With this riposte of 7 June 1952 Pollock described the past year's
activity that had seen a return to figuration with the pouring of black
oil and enamel paints onto raw cotton duck. A tissue of causes
underpinned the changes: the exhibition *Black or White* at the Kootz
Gallery in 1950 had popularized a revival of monochrome, Pollock's
psychological state grew sombre after Hans Namuth twice filmed
him in the private act of painting, and plans to incorporate his works
into a church project by the architect Tony Smith possibly revived his
ardour for ritualistic iconography. At any rate the 'black paintings',
dark in cast and feel, delve back to the nightmares a decade or more
beforehand but are invigorated by the technique of the previous four
years. They contain indications of recumbent presences with atten-
dants suggesting a deposition (*Number 14, 1951*) and single figures or
heads merged with serpentine snares (*Number 7, 1952*), except that the
absorbent ground and a very liquid medium create a spatiality quite
unlike the cosmic world of 1947–50. Here instead broods an
introspective realm whose phantasms appear locked *in* the support
rather than floating free. The analogy is to a blotting pad stained by a
reservoir of fearful disturbances seeping through from beneath. At the

137 Jackson Pollock *Number 14, 1951*

130   close of the sequence is the magisterial *Portrait and a Dream* (1953) which juxtaposes different signifiers in its two halves so that monochrome and colour, lines and plane, idealized self-portrait and inchoate tangle cohabit what amounts to a meditation on the structure of consciousness. Afterwards Pollock's personal decline abused his creativeness and the better works are more islands than links in a coherent chain. Pastiche occurs, though in an affecting way, with arguable allusions to Newman in the overwrought, hence belatedly

129   restructured *Blue Poles* (1952), Matisse in *Easter and the Totem* (1953), Still in *The Deep* (1953) and his own 1946–47 style in *White Light* (1954). The legend that the fatal car crash on 11 August 1956 was suicide says less about Pollock's straits than does the fitful pulse of everything he did towards the end.

    Traumatic as that death was for Krasner, it did at least offer her the chance of an identity beyond her husband's shadow and the attendant restraints in a movement dominated by men. Tenacity even seemed to grip her 1950s paintings, making them sharper and tenser. The cut-and-thrust of collage suited them and with a nod towards Matisse's late *découpages* Krasner went from torn black-and-white paper compositions to organic medleys of canvas pieces, cut-out paper and paint strokes. *Lame Shadow* and *Stretched Yellow* from 1955 resonate with tans, black and orange. But a further cycle beckoned next. A last vehement address to the now absent Pollock, it culminated in the frieze of *Another Storm* (1963) that shatters rhythms sprung from his universe into a filigreed avalanche. Lush harmonies re-emerged next alongside a decorativeness that by the 1970s drew upon Celtic, Islamic and natural sources. Then in a brave move she anatomized her own

138   history and in 1976 put knife or scissors to entire portfolios of studies kept since the 1930s, exemplifying a late Abstract Expressionist tendency to return to beginnings via a lifetime's perspective. Forms of the verb 'to be' gave titles to this series whose grainy charcoal revenants are spliced between bright gaps and shards in an architectonics worthy of Piranesi. Though Krasner was infirm and died in 1984 these kaleidoscopic vistas have the drive of someone rejuvenated who wrenches distant things back into the here and now.

    In the long term Siskind, de Kooning, Guston and Smith weathered their doldrums in the 1950s by balancing self-sufficiency with leaps into unexpected regions whereas Rothko, Still, Reinhardt and even Newman conducted themselves with a rather formidable singlemindedness. The later careers of the first four bring to mind the outgoing circles made by a stone cast into water and of the second

138 Lee Krasner *Diptych* 1977–78

more the trajectory of an arrow. One tended to elude finalities, while
the other sought them. Many Rothkos and Stills from the 1960s have
the solemnity of a testament but the equivalent de Kooning and a *Zig*
by Smith are prone to be wayward and ebullient.

Dogma slowed Siskind's success similarly to Krasner's. Here it
stemmed from the relative conservatism of photographic thought
which his own contribution helped to alter, especially after the 1959
monograph *Aaron Siskind: Photographs* appeared. But was Siskind
himself prey to lingering doubts about the medium's autonomy?
Both the anomalous figurative *Pleasures and Terrors* series and the   140
recurrence of quite forthright natural objects like stones, leaves and
trees would imply it. Perspective and more conventional lighting also
rendered some of his architectural views and plant studies compara-
tively orthodox. Yet instead of vitiating Siskind this passing 'naturalism' brought a fresh life to other photographs whose synthesis has
reached down to the present. Upon the stark ground resolved in the
late 1940s' pictures they elaborate fine and rapt nuances. If *Chicago 224,*   139
1953 again celebrates a forlorn building fragment it adds new layers of
transparency via the glass pane, kinaesthetic detail in the torn paper
and social unease (the graffiti). Or the scope of *St Louis 9, 1953* is

177

expanded to initiate a border of sky which heralds the framing motifs, mysterious shifts in scale and an otherworldly light that characterize his opus since the 1960s. His latest quarter of a century was anyway an odyssey whose dimensions encompassed the statuary and other relics of civilization's passage in the Roman studies (1963/67), an attention to surfaces that redefines the photography–painting dialectic in the *Homage to Franz Kline* sequence (1972–75), essays in chiaroscuro, and landscape as a metaphor for human tragedy in the visceral lava of the Hawaiian *Volcano* series (1980).

139 Aaron Siskind *Chicago 224, 1953*

140 Aaron Siskind
*Pleasures and Terrors
of Levitation 37, 1953*

With Pollock gone, *Woman I* elevated to a famous icon and gesturalism popularized, de Kooning received the somewhat premature mantle of 'Old Master'. In our era that has too often meant fossilization so that for him, as with the late Picasso, much has depended upon staying fresh and open. Ambiguity provided one panacea: 'That's what fascinates me – to make something that you will never be sure of, and no one else will either' (1972). Sexiness and humour beam from the portrayals of women especially, though still offset by a perennial expressionism seen in the 1969 graphic suite based upon Bruegel's allegorical *Blind leading the Blind*. Another side has waxed lyrical to leaven the existential ire. Noting the artist's summers in Long Island from 1951 on, critics sometimes read the six *Women* of the period as bathers in sun-filled watery settings whose azure, verdant and creamy tones sparkle about their bulk. This misses their angst yet catches what an unfinished *Woman as Landscape* (1955) confirms: an uplift in spirits attuned to the pastoral. Even the 1955–56 'urban landscapes' reflect it for they are the later 1940s *film noir* vision transformed, bursting into colour and with the former's sharp silhouettes now richly broken. Outward expansion propels the Abstract Parkway and Pastoral Landscapes (1957–61; 1960–63) of which de Kooning mentioned 'landscapes and highways and sensations . . . outside the city – with the feeling of going to the city or coming from it'. Influenced by Kline, these give painterliness its due, redeeming the brushstroke to sweep over them so that air, luminosity and speed prevail. After a permanent move to East Hampton in 1961 the geography of its Atlantic site, of pigment and of the body, blend. Here the *genii loci* are 'light floozies', or those who straddle the swell like the *Clam Diggers* (1964) and a 1975 title drawn from Keats's epitaph (. . . *Whose Name Was Writ in Water*) captures the mood of oceanic reverie. Additives that included kerosene, mayonnaise and water itself enhanced these beautiful deliquescent oils, which were further textured by paper or vellum pressed to them while wet. Space coagulates then shimmers with reflections before breaking apart, rather as nature's canopy itself had done for Monet at Giverny. This implicit tactility next materialized in twenty-five sculptures between 1969 and 1974. With bodies kneaded to a tragi-comic dough, their forebears are the passages where Rodin seems almost inflamed by the stubborn clay itself. Erotic tints and curves out of *Pink Angels* returned during the 1970s as likely signs that de Kooning was again on a pendulum swing between abstraction and the human presence, until ill health ended his activity as an artist around 1990.

133

141

When Smith's truck overturned on a Vermont road in 1965 it marked the third in a quartet of violent deaths extending from Gorky's and Pollock's and ahead to Rothko's suicide in 1970. Smith alone stood at a peak of ambition and productivity – some fifteen last years of maturity, rather than a 'late' phase, when he worked on a scale that once he had merely dreamt of. In an abandoned factory at Voltri in Italy in 1962 (and funded by the state steel company) he completed twenty-six large weldings in thirty days and the second of three *Wagons* from 1964 weighed around eight tons. He populated the fields outside the studio above Lake George in upstate New York with this progeny until they became an autobiographical environment. Apart from several hundred graphics and paintings each year Smith also used different sculptural idioms concurrently so that no neat synopsis fits them. He had always wanted this; after 1950 every prerequisite was right.

Firstly, his image–symbols were refined to types, faint yet compelling atavisms within ever more abstract, complex or improvisatory variants. Whether in the *Agricolas* (1951–59) using old farm implements, the ten *Tank Totems* (1952–60) with their boiler-tank

141 Willem de Kooning *Untitled XII*, 1982

ends, the brightly painted *Zigs* and *Circles* (1961–63 and 1962–63), the rust patined *Voltri-Boltons* (1962–63) or the burnished stainless steel *Cubi* (1961–65), various familiar motifs recur. There are solitary, heroic and spectral protagonists; disc and projecting shapes perhaps kin to the previous sexual imagery; grandly processional, archaic chariots; and tableaux of aerial forms that include stars and suns. Secondly, welding became his primary means and, after changing to the ultra-direct arc method during the 1950s, enabled him to join constituent parts with ease. These metal sheets, found objects and so forth he pushed around on the floor ('toeing in') like the planes of a collage almost as spontaneously as Pollock had painted in 1947–50. This led to working in series and to a celebration of both his encounter

142

with the materials and a pictorial frontality about the results. They are the climax of a lifetime's constructivist ideals, monuments to poise and placement yet with the semblance of having been daringly flung together.

All-inclusiveness had become Smith's goal. We see it in the multipartite *Volton XVIII* (1963) which brings a painter's contrapuntal imagination to bear upon a mechanistic and somehow quizzical object. Such pieces are hybrids of media (for spray drawings or graphics were often a starting-point), figural associations and industrial methods. If the *Sentinels* (1956–61) and several *Cubi* retain an upright core then *Zig IV* (1961) is all exterior, all surfaces in collision that defy any single viewpoint. Others float aloft resembling solidified Abstract Expressionist brushmarks, whereas the wheeled assemblages and *Wagons* are the apotheosis of a fascination with a sculpture's base,

142 David Smith *Wagon I* 1963–64

143 David Smith *Cubi XVIII, XVII and XIX* 1963, 1964

just as his experiments with polychromy, evocative rusty patinas and
the way the *Cubi* dissolve into a shining dazzle address the question of
its 'skin'. There is a 1960s sleekness about the *Cubi* due to their blocks,
cylinders and 'cushions' having been prefabricated of extremely hard
T-304 steel. Each of the twenty-eight has the largeness to hold its own
against sky, land and sun. Altogether perhaps three sub-groups occur.
Cubi XVIII and *XIX* (1964) picture colossal upraised still-lifes as 143
against the more anthropomorphic ones which embody an active
tense like metaphors of rising (*II*, 1962), pivoting (*VI*, 1963) and
striding (*XXIII*, 1964), which in turn complement the sublimely still
'gates' (*XXIV*, 1964) whose framing portals aspire to the architectural
– that threshold Rothko's late murals also explored – where our space
mediates other realms. Though the series was unfinished at Smith's
death he had already changed the course of twentieth-century
sculpture.

Smith's departure in the midst of his singular revolution spared him
the aftermath when less radical cadres frequently win acclaim. This
happened first in painting anyway and amongst the estranged old
guard were Newman, Rothko and Still. Few could comprehend the
gap between such austere paintings and the metaphysical claims they

183

made for them. Gesturalism had more appeal and was better grist to the mill of the existential rhetoric of the 1950s. As an avant-garde the trio also passed from being too advanced at first to relegation by the 1960s into forerunners of the more dispassionate abstract art of a younger generation. By a bitter stroke of irony Rothko's first two public commissions were for dining-rooms, Newman endured critical neglect and had a heart attack in 1957 and Still secluded himself before leaving New York for Maryland in 1961. Consequently their distance from an audience – plus the aspirations to reach one – had more effect than is usually thought. Content and communication *had* to be reasserted and an apocalyptic note crept in (Rothko: 'I'm interested only in expressing basic human emotions – tragedy, ecstasy, doom') which assumed that art hung somewhere in the balance between life and death. The visual repercussions were subtler and best summarized as that concentrated temper which sometimes accompanies introversion. All the same, failures became no less spectacular than achievements where more was wrung from less.

The magnetism of Newman's fourteen monochrome *Stations of the Cross* (1958–66) grows from their being outwardly plain. We are taken aback to encounter any religious *concetto* Here, then struck by the rightness: an iconoclasm indicative of last things; blacks hostile, at ebb,

144 Barnett Newman *Broken Obelisk* 1963–67

145 Barnett Newman *First Station* 1958

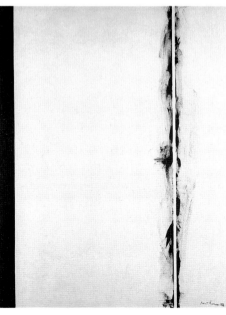

and in the *First Station* (1958) like tongues of flame that carve a 'zip' 145
from nothing. The serial format fosters meaning insofar as expression
depends on variations within an idiom (as Ernst Gombrich observes, a
Haydn dissonance might go unremarked in Schoenberg) and against
the sparse syntax throughout all fourteen stages every nuance tells.
Cross-references create a network which each beholder is free to
structure into his or her own ensemble. Newman's verdict on the
lithographic suite *18 Cantos* created towards the end (1963–64) of the
Stations applies alike to both: 'Each is separate. Each can stand by itself.
But its fullest meaning, it seems to me, is when it is seen together with
the others.' In miniature the measured intervals and solid crayon hues
of the lithographs foretold a certain diamond-brightness about his
next and latest paintings which significantly favoured acrylics.
'Absolute' was Newman's word for their enormous chromatic spans
energized by the narrowest margins (*Anna's Light* of 1968 is 9 × 20
feet) or by asymmetry (the triangular *Jericho*, 1968–69). None,
however, outshone the sculpture *Broken Obelisk* (1963–67). Its two 144
masses, both ancient symbols of humanity's address to space and time,
taper to an infinitesimal union while a concealed base lifts them just
above an earthly plane. As with Smith's *Cubi*, the ethos is Abstract
Expressionism at its purest, fusing concrete and transcendent levels.

146 Clyfford Still *Oil on Canvas July 1974*

After Still died in 1980 his reputation went into an unjustified eclipse rather like Newman's until the latter appeared to affirm Minimalist, Hard-Edge and other emergent 1960s trends. Only Still in old age remained the outsider, his huge pictorial fields with their ragged contours instantly recognizable phenomena unto themselves. The graphics have yet to be properly known. There was no particular turning-point although by 1956 the coagulated surfaces had lifted somewhat, piercing contrasts made bare canvas (whose liberation he had pioneered around 1950) register as a silvery continuum and in alliance with wider formats brought release. Yet old ghosts lingered everywhere: memories of revelatory flashes, petrified phantasms, silhouettes and abysses, all held like flies in the amber of abstraction. In one recurrent composition that ran from the famous *1957-D-No. 1* to 146 *Oil on Canvas July 1974* this unique mix of modernity and tradition came to the fore. There Still conferred spartan flatness upon an organizational logic that would not be amiss in Géricault's *Raft of the Medusa*. In another vein he left *Oil on Canvas June 3, 1970* largely untouched apart from the merest embers answering white and blue across silences which could be compared to those of American Luminism had not Still long since noted such measure in Cézanne and devoted half a century to this quickening of the void. Several of these conclusive pictures count amongst the most exhilarating of their time.

Now much the same Nietzschean sensibility took quite another turn in Rothko towards the tragic. His initial faith in the viewer's openness evidently waned and the paintings appeared to harden over the second half of the 1950s. Their spectra narrowed, growing either dim or more polarized, and the atmosphere was overcast in the commanding, even operatic *Four Darks in Red* (1958). This monumentality was in fact a dire rephrasing of his existing wish that the works be hung closely, low down on the wall and in a quite confined space so as to commune with the beholder. There would develop, that is, an osmosis between intimacy and environment. From here it was but a short step to the murals where private content and public setting could merge. Today we tend to remark their chequered histories, notably the fugitive Lithol Red pigment now faded to blue at Harvard and the once intrusive Texas sunlight in the Houston Chapel, only to forget how they consumed Rothko.

Murals called for different signifiers from the easel picture and Rothko evolved starker fields pitched in the crimson–oxblood–black scale with open centres (Seagram), keystone-like accents (Harvard) and triptychs (Houston). In this he also responded to sights on his intervening European trips of 1958 and 1966 including Pompeii's House of the Mysteries and its subfusc expanses of colour, the Fra

147

148

147 *left* Mark Rothko
Four Darks in Red 1958

148 Mark Rothko,
Houston Chapel, 1964–
67, the triptych at left

149 Mark Rothko
Untitled 1969

Angelicos and especially Michelangelo's Laurentian Library vestibule whose oppressive planes and recesses were probably long familiar from reproductions. Although the murals sometimes receive a narrow religious gloss (which supposes the uplifted central triptych section at Houston for example to 'represent' the Resurrection) this belies the artist's overriding fixation with the interplay between space and consciousness, now manifest as pictorial ensembles with the viewer bodily in their midst. Despite the asceticism his intent is human and universal enough to hark back at least to Leonardo's moment of awe in front of a dark cavernous threshold as recorded in the 'Notebooks'. Of the Seagram murals he said, 'I have made a place', and the Chapel transcends the merits of its individual images (where even his perennial and once fiery reds subside to a twilit state) to seek the archaic condition of a sanctuary and everything that implies in a secular culture. But where to go from there? Something of this fearsome prospect, now hard to separate from his depression, presided over the acrylics of 1968–69. A white border seals them off externally (the idea came from using masking tape around watercolours) while, within, blacks that remain uppermost to preclude landscape associations oppress never more than one sometimes turbulent grey zone. Studied negations of much that Rothko had held dear, they are saturated with the sense of an ending.

149

CHAPTER EIGHT

After Abstract Expressionism

The heritage of Abstract Expressionism is enormous. Like a text, it has filtered down to the present in many forms: in turn copied, creatively misread, extended beyond recognition, or flatly denied by its successors as when Robert Rauschenberg, in a neo-Dadaist mood, erased a de Kooning drawing he owned in 1952. That act attested to a chapter of history already written. Even our first sight of Pollock the artist–shaman who had internalized the age's forces and then expressed them in bodily actions now fits into a century-long progression. Its curve rises with the *fin-de-siècle* Dancer – Toulouse-Lautrec's lithograph of *Loïe Fuller* weaving whiplash patterns about herself – has Pollock near the apex, passes through the self-mutilations of the Austrian Performance artist Arnulf Rainer and sinks in Gilbert and George's stasis as 'living sculptures'. By then a critic such as Philip Leider could observe that 'it is as if his [Pollock's] work were the last achievement of whose status every serious artist is convinced' (1970).

The crucial stages in the movement's dissemination lasted until around 1960. After that any lessons tended to merge with everyday artistic practice. For painters the main result has been an expanded sensibility in three areas: scale, brushwork (or, more precisely, the mark-making process itself) and a franker declaration of the image as a total expanse or field. Such contemporaries as the German Anselm Kiefer or the American Julian Schnabel cannot be pigeonholed as heirs to Pollock, Still or others, yet their massive surfaces laden with psychic and cultural detritus and seething with evidence of the maker's powers – virtual fields of marks – are hard to envisage without those precedents and Schnabel has cited Newman's influence, saying his canvases 'were a palimpsest, a collection of signals that triggered an emotional and intellectual vision that resides in and outside of the painting.' A confrontational, iconic quality about much postwar art also derives to some extent from that historical watershed which certain large Abstract Expressionist works established by their frontal impact upon the beholder. Thus a cross-section of American painting around 1965 – Roy Lichtenstein's Pop icons, Kenneth Noland's hard-

150, 151

152

189

150 *top* Anselm Kiefer *Maikäfer flieg (Cockchafer, fly)* 1974

151 Julian Schnabel *Humanity Asleep* 1982

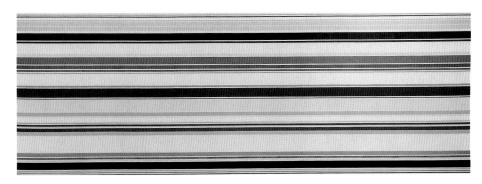

152 Kenneth Noland *Via Blues* 1967

edged chromatic abstractions and the more realistic yet larger-than-life portraits of Alex Katz or Philip Pearlstein's figures (cut by the frame in a manner indebted to Kline's compositions) – would for all the differences display this one common inheritance. Even David Hockney's placing of a careful 'gestural' splurge against a colour field in such pictures as *A Bigger Splash* (1967) revealed a sly awareness of where those extremes had originated. Scarcely any artist of his generation could not have known about the signifying force of paint and touch that was central to Abstract Expressionism.

At a superficial level 'gesturalism' comprised a set of pictorial devices for emulators on the international scene during the 1950s and amounted to a rhetoric of the splash and dribble in the theatrical hands of, for example, Georges Mathieu in France and the samurai-like displays (with brush rather than sword) of the Gutaï group of Japan; or it married more authentic native talents of the order of Alan Davie's in England whose offspring were his Celtic and mystical revisions of Pollock in the early 1940s. A renewed virility of attack to British painting during the later 1950s – one thinks of Roger Hilton and Peter Lanyon – is unlikely without the influx of Abstract Expressionism which was first properly seen there at the Tate Gallery in 1956. It also held a storehouse of forms that could be taken out of context and transposed from one medium to another, especially sculpture, since they appeared hard to extend in any pictorial sense. Thus the American sculptor Ibram Lassaw's rectilinear constructions became 153 more labyrinthine and encrusted with dribbled metal after 1950 in response to Pollock's catalytic style. Of the next generation John Chamberlain's assemblages employing crushed automobile parts and Mark di Suvero's angular timber and steel structures respectively 154

191

153 *left* Ibram Lassaw *Monoceros* 1952

154 Mark di Suvero *Hankchampion* 1960

materialize de Kooning's convoluted brushstroke and Kline's heavy vectors in three dimensions.

Once mythicized, Abstract Expressionism attracted an array of avant-gardist half-truths around itself – illustrated by Rosenberg's essays according to which 'risk', 'self-discovery', 'the new', 'voyaging into the unknown' and related existential shibboleths were its basic concerns. While these readings had some basis in the artists' statements they offered a model which suited a postwar American counter- or sub-culture that included the Beat generation and to whom Pollock became a cult hero, a counterpart to the intuitively driven 'bebop' jazz musicians like Charlie Parker and 'Dizzy' Gillespie, who had also spun out a stream of consciousness in melodic lines. Both Charles Olsen's conception of his poetry as an open field of energy and Jack Kerouac's improvisational writing methods ('sketching' in his words) developed around 1950–51 and were stimulated by Pollock's extemporizing approach. Another key figure in this context was Frank O'Hara, poet, curator at MoMA between 1960 and 1966 and friend of several Abstract Expressionists. To him they had shown how to exalt subjective experience and his 'Digression on "Number 1" 1948' (published in his 1959 Pollock monograph) elucidated this view in microcosm. Starting with factual statement the discourse suddenly alters at O'Hara's sight of the Pollock to a visionary and confessional mode. Elsewhere, his poetry's disrupted syntax, present tense and

155 Jasper Johns
Field Painting
1963–64

chance details are verbal analogues to the foregrounding of experience and texture by the painters he admired.

Although Abstract Expressionist music and dance would be misnomers, cross-influences extended to the composers Morton Feldman (1926–76), Earle Browne (1926–   ) and the choreographer Merce Cunningham (1919–   ). They were each again struck by what they perceived as a new spatiality which inspired Feldman to 'allow the sounds to be free' and evolve a graphic music notation around 1950–51 (the moment, indeed, of his score for the Pollock film) that articulated the idea of music as a colouring of time with strands of different pigment, a rationale relating to Guston's contemporary pictures like *Painting 1952*. Browne took this research into non-hierarchic sound towards an aural equivalent of the all-over composition when he presented *Folio* (1952–53), containing Pollock-like pieces for piano composed 'very rapidly and spontaneously and . . . in that sense performances rather than compositions.' He added that Pollock's working processes '*looked* like what I wanted to *hear* as sound'. The many innovations of Cunningham's dance style presupposed a fluency without specific climaxes or foci on the stage, which constitutes a non-hierarchic 'arena' or field akin to that of Rosenberg's American 'action painters', in which the dancers extemporize with the raw materials of their medium: empty space, time and bodily gesture.

Apart from Newman's plans for a synagogue, the house which Still built for himself in Alberta in 1946, and Rothko's passing collaboration with Philip Johnson on the Houston Chapel, no Abstract Expressionist branched into architecture proper despite their allusions to the humanization of space. The latter therefore probably accounts for the remarkable affinities between the buildings and thought of the American architect Louis Kahn (1901–74) and the attitudes of several figures in this book, most notably Newman and Rothko. Admittedly, nothing is yet known of Kahn's views, if any, about those contemporaries. Yet he pursued as they did over the same years elemental divisions of light and darkness, the structuring of an environment for an individual's spiritual uplift and the sense of 'place', all of which probably articulated as much a reaction against the anonymity of 1950s Establishment culture (encapsulated by the rapid American adoption of Mies's International Style that Still for one loathed) as it does their more obvious common Jewish humanist leanings. Certainly, Kahn's austere and monumental directness finds a response in the sublimities of postwar American painting more than in any architecture apart perhaps from Le Corbusier's brutalism. In his discipline Kahn occupied the parallel ground to Abstract Expressionism that Graham and Roethke did in dance and poetry.

The recent history of photography remains too multifarious and Siskind's contribution too up-to-the-minute for his long-term reputation to be made final. In its way that alone is a compliment. Yet already he can be seen to have enlarged, as did Minor White, the 'formalist' photographic tradition, reaching a pitch of abstraction allied to existential depths that were absent from its previous phases under László Moholy-Nagy, Edward Weston and Paul Strand. Moreover Siskind's resolve in exploring the regions where photography and painting contend and which had been a taboo issue at first even for White (as some reservations recorded in a private memo of 1954 reveal) found few peers. Through teaching at Chicago's Institute of Design and then the Rhode Island School of Design, Siskind's personal influence has also spread further afield via his students.

156 Louis Kahn, Kimbell Art Museum, Fort Worth, 1969–72 (Kahn himself in the auditorium)

157 *left* Helen
Frankenthaler *Mountains
and Sea* 1952

158 *below left* Morris Louis
Point of Tranquility
1959–60

159 *right* Helen
Frankenthaler *Blue
Territory* 1955

One of these, Roy Metzker, is noteworthy for his sparse field-like compositions that incorporate multiple prints.

The impressive variety of Smith's opus held out promises for several major channels in sculpture as it evolved from the 1950s onwards. Assemblage drew inspiration from his apotheosis of welding and fascination with the collage principle. Besides its exponents mentioned above like di Suvero and Chamberlain as well as the more surrealist and frequently humorous personages compiled by the American Richard Stankiewicz, the British sculptor Anthony Caro proved Smith's greatest debtor and thus a conduit of his influence. They had met in 1959 and the insights Caro gained led him to abandon modelling for welding and remark about Smith's late work that it 'showed me how to get away from . . . everything that constituted the "old look".' Simultaneously his enlightenment opened up possibilities never sought by his exemplar: painted steel constructions started in 1960 which express another altogether less romantic ideology no longer attuned to the body's placement and instead tending to be outlaid rather than uprisen, cool meditations on three-dimensionality.

160

160 *left* Anthony Caro *Early One Morning* 1962

161 Barry Flanagan *Large Leaping Hare* 1982

162 Walter Tandy Murch *Gear* 1950

163 Philip Guston *Ancient Wall* 1976

Aspects of Smith's pictorialism – the poetic, visionary and quizzical features that he adapted from the graphic arts – recurred in sculptors whose richer imagery ran counter to, or beyond, the Minimal and Conceptual austerities which prevailed from the later 1960s. As with the rethinking of the pedestal and use of multiple viewpoints, this is another area where his innovations have passed almost indistinguishably into the mainstream of twentieth-century sculptural practice but in numerous cases, whether the earlier charismatic entities of Philip King or the mythic hares presiding over the tableaux of Barry Flanagan, the spirit of Smith's tutelary sentinels and agile spectres continues. More questionable are the supposed connections between the *Cubi* and Minimalism's architectonic gestalts since the latter really

161

164 Robert Rauschenberg *Choke* 1964

belong instead to the circumstances that went with the disavowal, mining and revisions of Abstract Expressionism.

The possibility that the movement's ideas and techniques were applicable to subjects outside its preferred scope had existed almost from the start as proven by Walter Tandy Murch who studied under 162 Gorky in the late 1920s, exhibited thereafter at Betty Parsons and was admired by Newman and Rothko. Silence, frontality, layered textures and a mysterious inbuilt radiance to his paintings comprise Abstract Expressionist features that are directed upon otherwise everyday objects and machinery. Eschewed by almost everyone except de Kooning, this banality returned to engage a younger generation whose attitudes were formed during the Cold War period itself rather than the 1930s and therefore often inverted the radical stances and machismo espoused by their predecessors. A cerebralism that leant upon Marcel Duchamp's ironies seems also to have been stimulated by the composer–philosopher John Cage who spent long periods at the important locus for artists in the 1950s of Black Mountain College in North Carolina. In New York Cage linked up with an intellectual coterie that attracted O'Hara, Robert Rauschenberg and Jasper Johns.

Entire areas of Rauschenberg's and Johns's aesthetic are commentaries on the movement which was peaking during their student years and when their first mature efforts took shape as though it were a dead language ready for excavation or packaging. Too often this is interpreted as a straightforward reaction, underlined by Johns's often quoted remark, 'I don't want my work to be an exposure of my feelings', when actually it represented more an oblique critique, a handling of the selfsame alienation that deadened American life then and which produced such engaged artistic responses from others. Around 1949 Rauschenberg created all-white canvases and subsequently all-black descendants which put forward a neutered interpretation of those prototypes by Still and Newman who shared the same dealer, Betty Parsons. Here the observer's active role before the colour field is altered to a passive one, the plenum becomes an absence that awaits us. Instead of being absorbed or challenged by the surface, the onlooker's shadow merely falls across it. His subsequent 'combines' (1953–64) were literally built from pieces of the real world whereas Pollock and de Kooning had integrated their allusions, imagistic (de Kooning's 'no-environment') or actual (the foreign matter in *Full Fathom Five*) into a single tissue. At stake was a world view no longer yearning for unities. By introducing gestural marks devoid of a proper context Rauschenberg also negated their 'authentic' status as elements in a painterly network. *Choke* (1964) stratifies de Kooning's urban glimpses into colliding sign systems of paint (physically rendered) and silk-screened impressions (mechanically indexed). An even clearer instance of Abstract Expressionism recycled through conventions taken from the mass media was Lichtenstein's near contemporary *Brushstroke* series, unique personal traces become giant replicas in Ben-Day dots. Well beforehand, however, Johns had multiplied such ironic displacements and his *Field Painting* (1963–64) condenses a decade of them. Item by item, ideals from the past generation are processed into alien disguises: their symbolic chiaroscuro calls forth a light switch in a darkly painted passage (above left

164

155

202

165 Frank Stella *Arbeit Macht Frei* 1958

of centre), the encounter with materials yields several pots and brushes, lettering replaces noumenal chroma and depth gapes through a central break, the passive antitype of Newman's heroically virile 'zip'. Literary parallels to this replacement of a humanized vision by one of mirrored textual codes and signifiers were William Gaddis's novel *The Recognitions* (1955) and the overall drift into post-modernity announced in the fictions of John Barth and Thomas Pynchon (*V*, 1963).

Another retort to the recent past appeared with the first black paintings of Frank Stella shown at MoMA's *Sixteen Americans* in 1959 165 and then reinforced by his disclaimer: 'It [my painting] really is an object . . . What you see is what you see.' The sublime had been curtailed to factuality, to compositions where repetitive and hence self-referential patterns echoed the frame. We look *at* but not *into* them. Although Stella here swept metaphysics aside, he had adapted from Pollock the notion of a non-hierarchic image identified, more closely than Cubism had managed to do, with the literal picture plane, a quality elevated in the 1960s styles grouped under Greenberg's rubric of 'Post-Painterly Abstraction', the title of an essay published in 1964. Again these benefited from Abstract Expressionist insights and again the outcome was as much a criticism as a furtherance. Greenberg's writings did more than chronicle this process since he counselled Morris Louis, Noland and Jules Olitski on a personal level.

Greenberg's writings such as the didactic 'After Abstract Expressionism' (1962) at once analyse and predict what his artist–friends painted with an impeccable if historicist logic that also determined their practice. All subscribed to a Modernist belief that the previous movement had, in true avant-garde fashion, to be purified. According to Greenberg its essences were those peculiar to the medium but not yet denuded of everything extraneous so as to leave colour, flatness and openness triumphant. Louis moved in this direction first, some ten months after he saw *Mountains and Sea* (1952) by Helen Frankenthaler in 1953. An admirer of the Venetians, Frankenthaler's talent has since been to give Abstract Expressionism a joyous *coloratura* and in this picture, executed after visiting the Nova Scotia coast, she thinned down Pollock's poured paint into limpid watercolour-like washes. In his subsequent *Florals* and *Veils* series Louis applied her procedure to the newly developed acrylic pigments, soaking liquid colour into the canvas weave. In effect, therefore, he joined Pollock's graphic spontaneity with the glowing hue otherwise restricted to the chromatic field painters. Gains and losses accrued that apply to the Post-Painterly Abstraction of Noland and Olitski. The sheer evanescence competes with Rothko at his most sensuous, and Noland's stripes in chevron, horizontal and plaid arrangements are

157
159
158

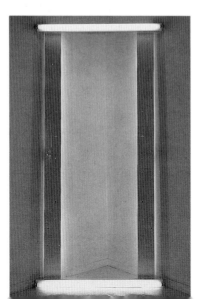

166 Dan Flavin *Untitled (Homage to Barnett Newman)* 1969

167 Brice Marden *Annunciation* 1978, installation view

defined with a more infinitesimal care than Newman's. Yet by comparison these paintings come across as hedonistic and less intensive, a Cythera of optical delights. Thus if they aspire to any broader tradition outside Greenberg's Modernism it might be one marginal to Abstract Expressionism, namely the pastoral, a dimension sometimes raised by Noland's titles with their allusions to nature and Olitski's admiration for the pearly light of Corot.

This splintering of our subject into impulses that took root like seeds far from their parent source increased as the art scene witnessed new movements arise at a breakneck pace and then become plurist by the start of the 1970s. The sublimely dramatic spaces declared by Newman, Still and Rothko returned as true environment in the installations of fluorescent lights by Dan Flavin and the epic   166 configurations hewn, raised and implanted on the American landscape ('earthworks') by Robert Smithson and Walter de Maria, whose *Lightning Field* (1971–77) in the Western desert is a Stillian hierarchy of sky, land and the sharp steel poles which are its vertical denizens. If Smithson surveyed the scorched Utah site of his *Spiral Jetty* (1970) and thought, by his own admission, of Pollock's *Eyes in the Heat*, then Brice Marden almost concurrently found in the Rothko mural cycles   167 and Newman's *Stations* a precedent for his planar oil and wax icons arranged in sequence to outlay an abstract spiritual narrative. In conflict with Marden's avowed 'Spartan limitations' stood the slightly earlier emergence of 'process' art identified with the sculpture of Eva Hesse, Robert Morris and the 'splash pieces' begun by Richard Serra in 1968 when molten lead was thrown against the angle between wall and floor. Not only did Pollock inspire Serra to make his bodily   168 energies generate the somewhat dangerous splashings but also the way that Process artists left materials to follow their own course – from Morris's felt strips disposed by gravity and Hesse's aleatory object groupings – drew on the Abstract Expressionists' regard for *techne* and especially their manipulation of chaos and flux which so impressed Hesse. But whether objecthood or dematerialization (the twin and divergent priorities of the 1960s and 1970s), each was moving beyond art practice as traditionally understood and in the changeover had deconstructed their models. To quote Alan Kaprow whose Happenings themselves accelerated the denouement: 'Pollock left us at the point where we must become preoccupied with and even dazzled by the space and objects of our everyday life.'

In the quiet privacy of the studio two artists had continued through these years to make paintings that restore faith in the medium's most fundamental powers. They were, of course, in at the start of the movement which had set the conditions for its very crisis. After Reinhardt's death in 1967 Frank Stella said, 'If you don't know what [his paintings] are about you don't know what painting is about.' What caused the remark were extraordinary dark canvases, five feet square and trisected into nine equal component squares, down to which by around 1960 he had eventually concentrated the preceding geometric works. He had needed half a lifetime to attain this purity, but it is a precarious one resonant with contradictions. The blackness proves ambiguous since the actual pigment was carefully adjusted to a velveteen light-absorbing mattness; the apparent monochrome is in fact of deepest shades of brown, blue and green; no brushstrokes can be seen yet they are manifestly done with intense care; even their

geometry recedes since the dimness almost effaces everything to a field. These 'ultimate' paintings (Reinhardt's own epithet) approach the bounds of perception – the last of Abstract Expressionism's demands upon the viewer – and embody art's mysterious otherness, the presence which Walter Benjamin called 'aura'.

What could be further from Reinhardt but still serve to remind us of another role for painting – its capacity to image and imagine – than the consequences of Philip Guston's volte-face in the year of his colleague's death? Unexpectedly he halted the palimpsest compositions which had grown greyed and more monumental by the early 1960s and instead wrenched to the surface scenes that they had seemed to cloak. His explanation was to the point: 'I got sick and tired of all that Purity! Wanted to tell Stories'; another earlier comment foretold their brushy, parodistic but infinitely judged manner: 'I should like to paint like a man who has never seen a painting, but this man, myself, lives in a world museum.' In effect Guston also resurrected more specific beginnings, those of the 1930s and 1940s but ever relevant to our wider existence: entropy in the scattered piles of useless and sometimes unnameable things that bulk large in these images like the dumb bedrock of consciousness, urban solitariness and political threat in the hooded Klansmen of *City Limits* (1969), presences reduced to bare signs of which the flat bootsoles (our lowest common denominators) amassed into the barrier and threshold of *Ancient Wall* remain a favourite. And between Reinhardt's abstract extremes and these provocative human traces roughly figured we see something of the span of Abstract Expressionism as well as its legacy to art that was then passing and still to come.

163

168 *left* Richard Serra
Splashing 1968

169 Ad Reinhardt
Abstract Painting No. 5
1962

Select Bibliography

With the literature on Abstract Expressionism already vast and steadily expanding the reader should pursue whatever aspects of it are best suited to his or her own special interests. The information here is therefore an initial key to further reading. Of the major studies, William C. Seitz, *Abstract Expressionist Painting in America* (Cambridge, MA, and London, 1983) and Irving Sandler, *Abstract Expressionism: The Triumph of American Painting* (New York and London, 1970) are important. The first, written as a PhD in 1955, contains information gathered from the artists themselves; the second was formerly a comprehensive account, but it is now dated and rivalled by Stephen Polcari, *Abstract Expressionism and the Modern Experience* (Cambridge and New York, 1991) and Michael Leja, *Reframing Abstract Expressionism* (New Haven and London, 1993). Dore Ashton, *The New York School: A Cultural Reckoning* (New York, 1973) reviews the social and aesthetic milieu of the movement. Leonard Walloch, ed., *New York: 1940–1965* (New York, 1988) does the same for New York City itself. Matthew Baigell, *The American Scene* (New York, 1974), Dickran Tashjian, *William Carlos Williams and the American Scene, 1920–1940* (New York, 1978) and Jeffrey Wechsler, *Surrealism and American Art, 1931–47* (New Brunswick, NJ, 1976) cover the early background period. Greta Berman and Jeffrey Wechsler, *Realism and Realities: The Other Side of American Painting 1940–1960* (New Brunswick, NJ, 1976) examines the alternatives to the Abstract Expressionist avant-garde during the Second World War and afterwards. Further useful exhibition catalogues (some of which reprint important articles) are: Maurice Tuchman, ed., *The New York School, The First Generation* (Los Angeles, 1965), Henry Geldzahler, *New York Painting and Sculpture: 1940–1970* (New York, 1969), Robert C. Hobbs and Gail Levin, *Abstract Expressionism: The Formative Years* (Ithaca, NY, 1978), E.A. Carmean Jr. *et al.*, *American Art at Mid-Century: The Subjects of the Artist* (Washington, D.C., 1978), Paul Schimmel, *The Interpretive Link: Abstract Surrealism into Abstract Impressionism* (Newport Beach, 1986), Kirk Varnedoe's essay in William Rubin, ed., *Primitivism in Twentieth Century Art* (New York, 1984) and Michael Auping *et al.*, *Abstract Expressionism: The Critical Developments* (New York and London, 1987). The last has both a chronology and an extensive bibliography listing monographs, articles and exh. cats. for all the painters in this book. *Art Journal* (Fall 1988) is devoted to Abstract Expressionism. Irving Sandler's *The New York School* (New York, 1978) and *American Art of the 1960s* (London, 1988) continues his survey of postwar American art into the 1960s.

Serge Guilbaut, *How New York Stole the Idea of Modern Art* (Chicago, 1983) represents the most ambitious yet largely unsatisfying attempt to examine the art's political implications; its bibliography notes the other writings in this field. Annette Cox, *Art-as-Politics: The Abstract Expressionist Avant-Garde and Society* (Ann Arbor, MI, 1982) fulfills a similar aim with greater success. Richard Pells, *Radical Visions and American Dreams: Culture and Social Thought in the Depression Years* (New York, 1973) explores the 1930s and its ideologies, and

Francis V. O'Connor, *Art for the Millions* (New York, 1973) documents the WPA. Introductory histories of the McCarthy years and after include David Caute, *The Great Fear* (London, 1978) and Marty Jezer's crude *The Dark Ages* (Boston, 1982). Douglas Miller and Marion Nowak, *The Fifties* (New York, 1977) offers a personal social memoir. Charles Harrison's condensed analysis of Abstract Expressionism overall appears in Nikos Stangos, ed., *Concepts of Modern Art* (London and New York, 1981). John O'Brian, ed., *Clement Greenberg: The Collected Essays and Criticism* (Chicago, 1986) reprints some of his brilliant writings; others are in Clement Greenberg, *Art and Culture* (Boston, 1961, and London, 1973). Harold Rosenberg's collected pieces include *The Tradition of the New* (New York, 1959), *The Anxious Object* (New York, 1964), *Art and Other Serious Matters* (Chicago, 1985) and *The De-Definition of Art* (London, 1972). Tom Wolfe, *The Painted Word* (New York, 1975) proves often funny and always silly. Lawrence Alloway's criticism is reprinted in his *Topics in American Art* (New York, 1975) and Robert Rosenblum leads the controversial 'sublime' interpretive trend with *Modern Painting and the Northern Romantic Tradition: Friedrich to Rothko* (New York, 1975, and London, 1978). Stewart Buettner, *American Art Theory, 1945–70* (Ann Arbor, MI, 1977) and Stephen C. Foster, *The Critics of Abstract Expressionism* (Ann Arbor, MI, 1980) chart the contemporary theorists and their critical framework. Russell Lynes, *Good Old Modern: An Intimate Portrait of the Museum of Modern Art* (New York, 1973) makes engaging reading.

The Abbeville Modern Masters series contains several well illustrated monographs including Elizabeth Frank, *Jackson Pollock* (New York, 1983), Harry Gaugh, *Willem de Kooning* (New York, 1983), Melvin Lader, *Arshile Gorky* (New York, 1985), Robert Storr, *Philip Guston* (New York, 1986) and Cynthia Goodman, *Hans Hofmann* (New York, 1986). The reader is referred to their bibliographies for further literature as well as to *Willem de Kooning: Paintings* (exh. cat., National Gallery of Art, Washington, D.C., 1994), the weighty *Jackson Pollock* (exh. cat., Centre Georges Pompidou, Musée National d'Art Moderne, Paris, 1982) and Ellen G. Landau's informative *Jackson Pollock* (New York and London, 1989). There are also three solid biographies: Steven Naifeh and Gregory White Smith, *Jackson Pollock: An American Saga* (New York, 1989); Nouritza Matossian's *Black Angel: A Life of Arshile Gorky* (London, 1998); and on Guston, by his daughter, Musa Meyer, *Night Studio* (New York, 1988). Catalogue raisonnés exist for Pollock, by Francis V. O'Connor and Eugene V. Thaw (New Haven, 1978), and for Gorky, by Jim Jordan and Robert Goldwater (New York, 1982). On Krasner the main monograph is Barbara Rose, *Lee Krasner: A Retrospective* (Houston and New York, 1983). H.H. Arnason, *Robert Motherwell* (New York, 2nd edn, 1982) is the most comprehensive single account. *Adolph Gottlieb: A Retrospective* (exh. cat., Corcoran Gallery of Art, Washington, D.C., 1981) is a helpful starting point. The same applies to Harry Gaugh, *Franz Kline, The Vital Gesture* (New York, 1985), otherwise rather bland. Thomas Hess, *Barnett Newman* (New York, 1971) remains a rich monograph, together with Brenda Richardson, *Barnett Newman: The Complete Drawings, 1944–1969* (Baltimore, 1979), Harold Rosenberg, *Barnett Newman: Broken Obelisk and Other Sculptures* (Seattle, 1971) and Hugh M. Davis and Riva Castleman, *The Prints of Barnett Newman* (Amherst, MA, 1983). Reinhardt's writings are anthologized by Barbara Rose, ed., *Art as Art: The Selected Writings of Ad Reinhardt* (New York, 1975); Lucy Lippard, *Ad Reinhardt* (New York, 1981) is thoughtful. My *Mark Rothko: The Works on Canvas – Catalogue Raisonné* (New Haven and London, 1998) is the starting point for all Rothko studies. Other key works of scholarship include Anna C. Chave, *Mark Rothko: Subjects in Abstraction* (New Haven, 1989), James E.B. Breslin: *Mark Rothko: A Biography* (Chicago and London, 1993) and Sheldon Nodelman, *The Rothko Chapel Paintings* (Austin, 1997). Still's donations to the Buffalo and San Francisco Museums are documented by Thomas Kellein, ed., *Clyfford Still: 1904–1980* (Munich, 1992). *Clyfford Still: Paintings 1944–1960* (exh. cat., Hirshhorn Museum, Washington, D.C.) is the latest contribution to the field. On Baziotes, see *William Baziotes: A Retrospective Exhibition* (Newport Beach, 1978); on Stamos, Ralph Pomeroy, *Stamos* (New York, 1974); and on Tomlin, *Bradley Walker Tomlin: A Retrospective View* (Garden City, NY, 1975).

Among the several good general views of postwar American photography are Jonathan Green, *American Photography: A Critical History, 1945 to the Present* (New York, 1984) and Peter Turner, ed., *American Images: 1945–1980* (exh. cat., Barbican Art Gallery, London, and Harmondsworth, Middlesex, 1985). These are afforded a wider context by *On the Art of Fixing a Shadow* (exh. cat., National Gallery of Art, Washington, D.C., 1989). Carl Chiarenza, *Aaron Siskind: Pleasure and Terrors* (Boston, 1982) is the primary reference and has an exhaustive bibliography.

200 Years of American Sculpture (exh. cat., Whitney Museum of American Art, New York, 1976), Wayne Andersen, *American Sculpture in Process: 1930/1970* (Boston, 1975) and Lisa Phillips, *The Third Dimension: Sculpture of the New York School* (New York, 1984) give a perspective on Smith. Both Karen Wilken, *David Smith* (New York, 1984) and Stanley E. Marcus, *David Smith: The Sculptor and his Work* (Ithaca, NY, 1983) are clear introductions with detailed references for further reading that balance Rosalind Krauss's provocative yet ultimately unconvincing thesis, *Terminal Iron Works: The Sculpture of David Smith* (Cambridge, MA, 1971) and Paul Cummings, *David Smith: The Drawings* (New York, 1979).

List of Illustrations

Measurements are given in centimetres then inches, height before width; a third figure indicates depth.

1 Jackson Pollock, 1950. Photo Hans Namuth, New York.
2 *Now there's a nice contemporary sunset! New Yorker* 29 November 1964. Drawing by Stevenson; © 1964 The New Yorker Magazine, Inc.
3 Jackson Pollock, 1949. Photo © Arnold Newman.
4 Norman Rockwell *Abstract and Concrete (The Connoisseur)*, 1962. *Saturday Evening Post* cover, 13 January 1962.
5 Jackson Pollock painting *No. 32* 1950. Photo Rudolph Burckhardt.
6 Mark Rothko *White Band (No. 27)* 1954. Oil on canvas, 220 × 205.7 (86⅜ × 81). Private Collection.
7 Barnett Newman in front of *Onement VI*. Photo Alexander Liberman, 1963.
8 Jackson Pollock *Self-Portrait c.* 1930–33. Oil on gesso on canvas, mounted on composition board, 18.4 × 13.3 (7¼ × 5¼). Courtesy the Jason McCoy Gallery, Inc, New York.

9 Arshile Gorky *Self-Portrait at the Age of Nine, c.* 1913 *c.* 1927. Oil on canvas, 30.5 × 25.7 (12 × 10½). Private Collection.
10 Clyfford Still *Self-Portrait* 1940. Oil on canvas, 105.4 × 96.5 (41½ × 38). Collection of the Estate of Clyfford Still. Photo Sandra Still.
11 Franz Kline *Red Clown* 1944. Oil on canvas, 59.7 × 50.8 (23½ × 20). Collection Mr and Mrs I. David Orr.
12 Mark Rothko *Self-Portrait* 1936. Oil on canvas, 81.9 × 66 (32¼ × 26). Copyright 1989 Kate Rothko Prizel & Christopher Rothko/ARS N.Y. Solomon R. Guggenheim Museum, New York. Photo Robert E. Mates and Mary Donlon.
13 Willem de Kooning *Woman I* 1950–52. Oil on canvas, 192.7 × 147.3 (75⅞ × 58). Collection, The Museum of Modern Art, New York. Purchase.
14 Ad Reinhardt *How to Look at Modern Art in America*, *P.M.*, 2 June 1946.
15 Charles Sheeler *Upper Deck* 1929. Oil on canvas, 74 × 56.3 (29⅛ × 22⅛). Harvard University, Cambridge, Mass., Louise E. Bettens Fund.

16 Charles Burchfield *Black Houses* 1936. Watercolour, 39.4×62.2 ($15\frac{1}{2} \times 24\frac{1}{2}$). Private Collection.
17 Edward Hopper *Sunday* 1926. Oil on canvas, 73.6×86.3 (29×34). The Phillips Collection, Washington, D.C.
18 Grant Wood *Spring Turning* 1936. Oil on masonite panel, 46×101.6 ($18\frac{1}{8} \times 40$). Private Collection.
19 Thomas Hart Benton *City Activities – Dance Hall* from *America Today* 1930. Distemper and egg temper on gessoed linen with oil glaze, 233.7×341.6 ($92 \times 134\frac{1}{2}$). © The Equitable Life Assurance Society of the United States, New York.
20 Jackson Pollock *Going West c.* 1934–38. Oil on gesso on composition board, 38.4×53 ($15\frac{1}{8} \times 20\frac{7}{8}$). National Museum of American Art, Smithsonian Institution, Washington, D.C., gift of Thomas Hart Benton.
21 J.M.W. Turner *Hannibal Crossing the Alps* 1812. Oil on canvas, 145×237.5 (57×93). Tate Gallery, London.
22 Jackson Pollock *Flame c.* 1934–38. Oil on canvas mounted on composition board, 51.1×76.2 ($20\frac{1}{2} \times 30$). Collection, The Museum of Modern Art, New York. Enid A. Haupt Fund.
23 Jackson Pollock *Camp with Oil Rig c.* 1930–33. Oil on gesso board, 45.7×64.4 ($18 \times 25\frac{3}{8}$). Mr and Mrs John W. Mecom, Jr. Photo Norlene Tips.
24 Clyfford Still *Houses at Nespelem* 1936. Oil on canvas, 55.9×71.1 (22×28). Collection Robert Sandberg.
25 Clyfford Still *Untitled ('Two Figures') c.* 1935–36. Oil on canvas, 122×96.5 (48×38). Private Collection.
26 Clyfford Still *Row of Grain Elevators* 1928. Oil on canvas, 87×112.9 ($34\frac{1}{4} \times 44\frac{1}{2}$). National Museum of American Art, Smithsonian Institution, Washington, D.C., gift of International Business Machines Corporation.
27 Franz Kline *Palmerton, Pa.* 1941. Oil on canvas, 53.5×69 ($21 \times 27\frac{1}{8}$). National Museum of American Art, Smithsonian Institution, Washington, D.C., Museum Purchase.
28 David Smith *Saw Head* 1933. Iron painted orange and brown, $46.4 \times 30.5 \times 21$ ($18\frac{1}{4} \times 12 \times 8\frac{1}{4}$). Courtesy the David Smith Papers, Archives of American Art, Smithsonian Institution, Washington, D.C. Photo David Smith.
29 David Smith *Medal for Dishonor No. 9: Bombing Civilian Populations* 1939. Bronze cast. Courtesy the David Smith Papers, Archives of American Art, Smithsonian Institution, Washington, D.C.
30 Philip Guston *Conspirators* 1932. Oil on canvas, 127×91.4 (50×36). Unlocated. Courtesy The Estate of Philip Guston. Photo Robert E. Mates.
31 Mark Rothko *Subway Scene* 1938. Oil on canvas, 85.7×116.8 ($33\frac{3}{4} \times 46$). Copyright 1989 Kate Rothko Prizel & Christopher Rothko/ARS N.Y. Solomon R. Guggenheim Museum, New York. Photo Robert E. Mates and Mary Donlon.
32 Mark Rothko *Interior* 1936. Oil on hardboard, 60.7×46.5 ($23\frac{7}{8} \times 18\frac{1}{4}$). National Gallery of Art, Washington, D.C. Gift of the Mark Rothko Foundation, Inc.
33 Paul Strand *Wall Street, New York, 1915*. Platinum photographic print (mercury toned), 24.8×32.3 ($9\frac{3}{4} \times 12\frac{3}{4}$). Collection Centre Canadien d'Architecture/Canadian Centre for Architecture, Montreal. Photo copyright © 1971, Aperture Foundation, Inc., Paul Strand Archive.
34 Aaron Siskind *Dead End: The Bowery* 1937. Photograph. Courtesy Aaron Siskind.
35 Willem de Kooning *Man c.* 1939. Oil on paper, mounted on composition board, 28.6×24.8 ($11\frac{1}{4} \times 9\frac{3}{4}$). Private Collection, New Orleans.
36 Walker Evans *Subway Portrait* 1938–41. Gelatin-silver print 17.8×18.8 ($7 \times 7\frac{3}{8}$). The Museum of Modern Art, New York. Purchase.
37 Philip Guston *Bombardment* 1937–38. Oil on wood, 116.8 (46) diameter. Courtesy The Estate of Philip Guston. Photo Robert E. Mates.
38 Philip Guston *If This Be Not I* 1945. Oil on canvas, 107.6×140.3 ($42\frac{3}{8} \times 55\frac{1}{4}$). Washington University Gallery of Art, St Louis, University Purchase, Kende Sale Fund, 1945.
39 Hans Hofmann *Table With Teakettle, Green Vase, Red Flowers* 1936. Oil on canvas, 138.4×102.6 ($54\frac{1}{2} \times 40\frac{3}{8}$). University Art Museum, University of California at Berkeley. Gift of the Artist. Photo Benjamin Blackwell.
40 Lee Krasner *Nude Study from Life* 1940. Charcoal on paper, 62.9×48.3 ($24\frac{3}{4} \times 19$). Robert Miller Gallery, NY.
41 Arshile Gorky *Organization* 1933–36. Oil on canvas 127.6×153.5 ($50\frac{1}{4} \times 60\frac{1}{4}$). National Gallery of Art, Washington, D.C. Ailsa Mellon Bruce Fund.
42 Pablo Picasso *Seated Woman* 1927. Oil on wood, 130×97 ($51\frac{1}{8} \times 38\frac{1}{4}$). Collection, The Museum of Modern Art, New York. Fractional gift of James Thrall Soby.
43 Arshile Gorky *Night-time, Enigma and Nostalgia c.* 1930–32. Ink on paper, 61×78.7 (24×31). Collection of Whitney Museum of American Art, New York. 50th Anniversary gift of Mr and Mrs Edwin A. Bergman, 80.54.
44 Arshile Gorky *The Artist and his Mother c.* 1926–34. Oil on canvas, 152.4×127 (60×50). Collection of Whitney Museum of American Art, New York. Gift of Julien Levy for Maro and Natasha Gorky in memory of their father, 50.17.
45 Willem de Kooning *Seated Figure (Classic Male)* 1939. Oil and charcoal on plywood, 138.2×91.4 ($54\frac{3}{8} \times 36$). Private Collection.
46 Willem de Kooning *Elegy c.* 1939. Oil and charcoal on composition board, 102.2×121.6 ($40\frac{1}{4} \times 47\frac{7}{8}$). Private Collection.
47 Robert Motherwell *The Little Spanish Prison* 1941–44. Oil on canvas, 69.2×43.5 ($27\frac{1}{4} \times 17\frac{1}{8}$). Collection, The Museum of Modern Art, New York. Gift of Renate Ponsold Motherwell.
48 Aaron Siskind *Chilmark 1940*. Photograph. Courtesy Aaron Siskind.
49 Mark Rothko *Untitled* 1939–40. Oil on canvas, 75.6×91.4 ($29\frac{3}{4} \times 36$). Copyright 1989 Kate Rothko Prizel & Christopher Rothko/ARS N.Y. Photograph courtesy the Pace Gallery, New York.
50 Ad Reinhardt *No. 30, 1938*. Oil on canvas, 102.9×108 ($40\frac{1}{2} \times 42\frac{1}{2}$). Collection of Whitney Museum of American Art, New York. Promised gift of Mrs Ad Reinhardt. P. 31.77.
51 Clyfford Still *1938–N–No. 1*. Oil on canvas, 78.6×64 ($30\frac{7}{8} \times 25\frac{1}{4}$). San Francisco Museum of Modern Art. Gift of the Artist.
52 David Smith *Interior for Exterior* 1939. Steel and bronze, $45.7 \times 55.9 \times 84.5$ ($18 \times 22 \times 33\frac{1}{4}$). Private Collection.
53 Jackson Pollock *Panel with Four Designs c.* 1934–38. Oil on masonite, 19.6×68.5 ($7\frac{3}{4} \times 27$). Courtesy Jason McCoy Gallery, Inc, New York.
54 Jackson Pollock *Naked Man with Knife c.* 1938–41. Oil on canvas, 127×91.4 (50×36). Tate Gallery, London.
55 Jackson Pollock, sketchbook study, *c.* 1938–39. Pencil and coloured crayon on paper, 35.6×25.4 (14×10). Private Collection.
56 Adolph Gottlieb *Eyes of Oedipus* 1941. Oil on canvas, 81.9×63.5 ($32\frac{1}{4} \times 25$). © 1979 Adolph and Esther Gottlieb Foundation, New York.
57 Mark Rothko *Slow Swirl at the Edge of the Sea* 1944. Oil on canvas, 191.4×215.3 ($75\frac{3}{8} \times 84\frac{3}{4}$). Collection, The Museum of Modern Art, New York. Bequest of Mrs Mark Rothko through the Mark Rothko Foundation, Inc.

58 Adolph Gottlieb *Masquerade* 1945. Oil and tempera on canvas, 91.4 × 61 (36 × 24). © 1979 Adolph and Esther Gottlieb Foundation, New York.
59 Jackson Pollock *Guardians of the Secret* 1943. Oil on canvas, 123.8 × 190.5 ($48\frac{3}{4}$ × 75). San Francisco Museum of Modern Art. Albert M. Bender Collection. Albert M. Bender Bequest Fund Purchase.
60 Richard Pousette-Dart *Symphony No. 1, The Transcendental* 1942. Oil on canvas, 228.5 × 304.7 (90 × 120). Collection of the Artist.
61 Arshile Gorky *The Liver Is the Cock's Comb* 1944. Oil on canvas, 186 × 250 ($73\frac{1}{4}$ × $98\frac{3}{8}$). Albright-Knox Art Gallery, Buffalo, New York. Gift of Seymour H. Knox.
62 Clyfford Still *July–1945–R*. Oil on canvas, 175.3 × 81.3 (69 × 32). Albright-Knox Art Gallery, Buffalo, New York. Gift of the Artist, 1964.
63 Jackson Pollock *Male and Female c.* 1942. Oil on canvas, 184.4 × 124.5 (73 × 49). Philadelphia Museum of Art. Partial gift of Mrs H. Gates Lloyd.
64 Bradley Walker Tomlin *Number 9: In Praise of Gertrude Stein* 1950. Oil on canvas, 124.5 × 259.8 (49 × $102\frac{1}{4}$). Collection, The Museum of Modern Art, New York. Gift of Mrs John D. Rockefeller 3rd.
65 Aaron Siskind *Martha's Vineyard (Seaweed) 2* 1943. Photograph. Courtesy Aaron Siskind.
66 Robert Motherwell *Pancho Villa Dead and Alive* 1943. Gouache and oil with collage on cardboard, 71.1 × 91.1 (28 × $35\frac{7}{8}$). Collection, The Museum of Modern Art, New York. Purchase.
67 Jared French *The Sea* 1946. Egg tempera, 62.2 × 91.4 ($24\frac{1}{2}$ × 36). Unlocated. Photo Victor Pustai, courtesy of the Jane Voorhees Zimmerli Art Museum, Rutgers, The State University of New Jersey, New Brunswick, New Jersey.
68 Theodoros Stamos *Ancestral Myth*, 1947. Oil on masonite, 61 × 76.2 (24 × 30). Photo Steve Lopez, courtesy Louis K. Meisel Gallery, New York.
69 Mark Rothko *Untitled* 1945–46. Watercolour on paper, 103.5 × 69.2 ($40\frac{3}{4}$ × $27\frac{1}{4}$). National Gallery of Art, Washington, D.C. Gift of the Mark Rothko Foundation, Inc.
70 Barnett Newman *The Death of Euclid* 1947. Oil on canvas, 40.6 × 50.8 (16 × 20). Private Collection.
71 Aaron Siskind *Gloucester 16A, 1944*. Photograph. Courtesy Aaron Siskind.
72 Mark Rothko *The Syrian Bull* 1943. Oil on canvas, 100.3 × 69.9 ($39\frac{1}{2}$ × $27\frac{1}{2}$). Reproduced courtesy of Annalee Newman insofar as her rights are concerned.
73 David Smith *War Spectre* 1944. Painted steel, 36.8 × 57.5 × 17.1 ($14\frac{1}{2}$ × $22\frac{5}{8}$ × $6\frac{3}{4}$). The Museum of Fine Arts, Houston. Museum Purchase.
74 David Smith *Window's Lament* 1942. Forged and fabricated steel and bronze, 34.3 × 50.8 × 17.5 ($13\frac{1}{2}$ × 20 × $6\frac{5}{8}$). Private Collection.
75 Jackson Pollock *Mural* 1943–44. Oil on canvas, 243.2 × 602 ($95\frac{3}{4}$ × $237\frac{1}{2}$). The University of Iowa Museum of Art. Gift of Peggy Guggenheim.
76 Arshile Gorky *Waterfall c.* 1943. Oil on canvas, 153.7 × 113 ($60\frac{1}{2}$ × $44\frac{1}{2}$). Tate Gallery, London.
77 Clyfford Still *Untitled 1946*. Oil on canvas, 156.9 × 113 ($61\frac{3}{4}$ × $44\frac{1}{2}$). The Metropolitan Museum of Art, New York, Arthur Hoppock Hearn and George A. Hearn Funds, 1977 (1977.174).
78 Mark Rothko *Number 18 c.* 1948. Oil on canvas, 154.9 × 109.9 (61 × $43\frac{1}{4}$). National Gallery of Art, Washington, D.C. Gift of the Mark Rothko Foundation, Inc.
79 Barnett Newman *Untitled* 1947. Ink, 27.3 × 11.4 ($10\frac{3}{4}$ × $4\frac{1}{2}$). Reproduced courtesy of Annalee Newman insofar as her rights are concerned.
80 Franz Kline *Four Studies* 1945–47. Ink and oil on paper, 18.4 × 18.4 ($7\frac{1}{4}$ × $7\frac{1}{4}$). Mrs E. Ross Zogbaum.
81 Franz Kline, study for *The Dancer* 1946. Ink, pastel, crayon and oil on paper, 17.8 × 7.6 (7 × 3). Collection Mr and Mrs I. David Orr.
82 Robert Motherwell *At Five in the Afternoon* 1949. Casein on composition board, 38.1 × 50.8 (15 × 20). Private Collection.
83 Aaron Siskind *New York I, 1947*. Photograph. Courtesy Aaron Siskind.
84 Aaron Siskind *Chicago (Auto Graveyard) 3, 1948*. Photograph. Courtesy Aaron Siskind.
85 David Smith *Oculus* 1947. Unlocated. Courtesy the David Smith Papers, Archives of American Art, Smithsonian Institution, Washington, D.C. Photo David Smith.
86 David Smith *The Letter* 1950. Welded steel, 90.5 × 58 × 23.5 ($35\frac{5}{8}$ × $22\frac{7}{8}$ × $9\frac{1}{4}$). Munson-Williams-Proctor Institute Museum of Art, Utica, New York.
87 Arshile Gorky *Agony* 1947. Oil on canvas, 101.6 × 128.3 (40 × $50\frac{1}{2}$). Collection, The Museum of Modern Art, New York. A. Conger Goodyear Fund.
88 Titian *Diana Surprised by Actaeon* (detail) 1556–59. Oil on canvas, 190 × 207 ($74\frac{3}{4}$ × $81\frac{1}{2}$). Duke of Sutherland Collection, on loan to the National Gallery of Scotland.
89 Willem de Kooning *Pink Angels c.* 1945. Oil and charcoal on canvas, 132 × 101.6 (52 × 40). Collection of the Frederick Weisman Company, Los Angeles, California.
90 Skater, *Life* 1945. Photo Gjon Mili, © Time Inc. 1945.
91 Hans Hofmann *Fantasia c.* 1943. Oil, duco, casein on plywood, 130.8 × 93 ($51\frac{1}{2}$ × $36\frac{5}{8}$). University Art Museum, University of California at Berkeley. Gift of the Artist.
92 Jackson Pollock *Number 1, 1948*. Oil on canvas, 172.7 × 264.2 (68 × 104.) Collection, The Museum of Modern Art, New York. Purchase.
93 Weegee *Coney Island, 4 p.m. July 28, 1940*. Photograph. The Weegee Collection.
94 Jackson Pollock *Eyes in the Heat* 1946. Oil on canvas, 137 × 109 (54 × 43). Private Collection.
95 Lee Krasner *Noon* 1947. Oil on linen, 61.3 × 76.2 (24 × 30). Courtesy Robert Miller Gallery, New York.
96 Jackson Pollock *Full Fathom Five* 1947. Oil on canvas with nails, tacks, buttons, key, coins, cigarettes, matches, etc., 129.2 × 76.5 ($50\frac{7}{8}$ × $30\frac{1}{8}$). Collection, The Museum of Modern Art, New York. Gift of Peggy Guggenheim.
97 Jackson Pollock *Tondo* 1948. Oil and enamel on metal 58.7 ($23\frac{1}{8}$) diameter. Private Collection, Illinois, courtesy Jason McCoy Gallery, Inc, New York.
98 Jackson Pollock, *Lavender Mist* 1950. Oil, enamel and aluminium on canvas, 221 × 299.7 (87 × 118). National Gallery of Art, Washington, D.C. Ailsa Mellon Bruce Fund.
99 Willem de Kooning *Light in August c.* 1946. Oil and enamel on paper mounted on canvas, 139.7 × 105.4 (55 × $41\frac{1}{2}$). Tehran Museum of Contemporary Art.
100 Bernard Perlin *Orthodox Boys* 1948. Tempera on board, 76.2 × 101.6 (30 × 40). Tate Gallery, London.
101 Willem de Kooning *Excavation* 1950. Oil and enamel on canvas, 203.2 × 254.3 (80 × 100). Mr and Mrs Frank G. Logan Purchase Prize, Gift of Mr and Mrs Noah Goldowsky and Edgar Kaufmann Jr, 1952.1. © 1989 The Art Institute of Chicago. All Rights Reserved.
102 Clyfford Still *1948–D*. Oil on canvas, 236.5 × 202.2 (93 × $79\frac{5}{8}$). Private Collection.
103 Clyfford Still *Untitled (Oil on Paper)* 1943. Oil on paper, 48.3 × 27.9 (19 × 11). Collection of Senator Frank R. Lautenberg. Photo Christie's, New York.

104 Clyfford Still *1948-E*. Oil on canvas, 208.3 × 175.3 (82 × 69). Albright-Knox Art Gallery, Buffalo, New York. Gift of the Artist, 1964.

105 Philip Guston *Porch II* 1947. Oil on canvas, 158.8 × 109.2 (62$\frac{1}{2}$ × 43). Munson-Williams-Proctor Institute Museum of Art, Utica, New York.

106 Philip Guston *The Tormentors* 1947–48. Oil on canvas, 103.9 × 153.7 (40$\frac{7}{8}$ × 60$\frac{1}{2}$). San Francisco Museum of Modern Art. Gift of the Artist.

107 Philip Guston, study for *The Tormentors* 1947. Ink wash on paper, 25.4 × 25.4 (10 × 10). Collection The Edward R. Brodia Trust, California.

108 Mark Rothko *Untitled* 1948. Oil on canvas, 134.9 × 118.4 (53$\frac{1}{8}$ × 46$\frac{5}{8}$). National Gallery of Art, Washington, D.C. Gift of the Mark Rothko Foundation, Inc.

109 Mark Rothko *Number 22 c.* 1949. Oil on canvas, 297 × 272 (117 × 107$\frac{1}{8}$). Collection, The Museum of Modern Art, New York. Gift of the Artist.

110 Barnett Newman *Cathedra* 1951, installation view, 1958. Photo Peter A. Juley and Son Collection, National Museum of American Art, Smithsonian Institution, Washington D.C.

111 Gardner Rea, 'One nice thing about television, you don't have to pick out where to look'. © 1951, 1979 The New Yorker Magazine, Inc.

112 Ad Reinhardt *Red Painting* 1952. Oil on canvas, 365.9 × 193 (144 × 76). The Metropolitan Museum of Art, New York, Arthur Hoppock Hearn Fund, 1968 (68–85).

113 Francisco Goya *Dog Buried in Sand* 1820–33. Oil on canvas, 134 × 80 (52.8 × 31.5). Museo del Prado, Madrid. Photo Mas.

114 Andrew Wyeth *Winter* 1946. Tempera on board, 79.7 × 121.9 (31$\frac{3}{8}$ × 48). North Carolina Museum of Art, Raleigh. Purchased with funds from the State of North Carolina.

115 Ben Shahn *Pacific Landscape* 1945. Tempera on paper on composition board, 64.1 × 99.1 (25$\frac{1}{4}$ × 39). Collection, The Museum of Modern Art, New York. Gift of Philip L. Goodwin.

116 Ben Shahn *Handball* 1939. Tempera on paper on composition board, 57.8 × 79.4 (22$\frac{3}{4}$ × 31$\frac{1}{4}$). Collection, The Museum of Modern Art, New York. Abby Aldrich Rockefeller Fund.

117 Aaron Siskind *Chicago* 1947–48. Photograph. Courtesy Aaron Siskind.

118 Philip Guston *Review* 1948–50. Oil on canvas, 100 × 149.9 (39$\frac{3}{8}$ × 59). Collection Musa Guston, Woodstock, New York.

119 Clyfford Still *Painting 1952*. Oil on canvas, 302.3 × 396.2 (119 × 156). Wirt D. Walker Fund, 1962.906. © 1989 the Art Institute of Chicago. All Rights Reserved.

120 Barnett Newman *Cathedra* 1951. Oil and magna on canvas, 244 × 541 (96 × 213). Stedelijk Museum, Amsterdam.

121 Barnett Newman *Onement I* 1948. Oil on canvas, 69 × 41 (27 × 16). Reproduced courtesy of Annalee Newman insofar as her rights are concerned.

122 Barnett Newman *The Wild* 1950, installation view. Oil on canvas, 243 × 4.1 (95$\frac{3}{4}$ × 1$\frac{5}{8}$). Collection, The Museum of Modern Art, New York. Gift of the Kulicke family.

123 David Smith *The Hero* 1951–52. Steel, 187.3 × 64.8 × 29.9 (73$\frac{3}{4}$ × 25$\frac{1}{2}$ × 11$\frac{3}{4}$). The Brooklyn Museum, New York, 57.185. Dick S. Ramsay Fund.

124 David Smith *Hudson River Landscape* 1951. Steel and stainless steel, 125.7 × 190.5 × 42.5 (49$\frac{1}{2}$ × 75 × 16$\frac{3}{4}$). Collection of Whitney Museum of American Art, New York.

125 Ad Reinhardt *Painting 1950*. Oil on canvas, 77.5 × 103 (30$\frac{1}{2}$ × 40$\frac{1}{2}$). Private Collection.

126 Philip Guston *Painting 1952*. Oil on canvas, 121.9 × 129.5 (48 × 51). Collection of Muriel Kallis Steinberg Newman. Photo Alan B. Newman, Chicago.

127 Mark Rothko *Untitled* 1954. Oil on unprimed canvas, 236.2 × 142.9 (93 × 56$\frac{1}{4}$). Yale University Art Gallery, The Katherine Ordway Collection.

128 State I of Willem de Kooning's *Woman I*, 1950. Photo Rudolph Burckhardt.

129 Jackson Pollock *Blue Poles* 1952. Enamel and aluminium paint with glass on canvas, 210.8 × 487.6 (83 × 92). Australian National Gallery, Canberra.

130 Jackson Pollock *Portrait and a Dream* 1953. Oil on canvas, 147.6 × 341.6 (58$\frac{1}{8}$ × 134$\frac{1}{2}$). Dallas Museum of Art. Gift of Mr and Mrs Algur H. Meadows and the Meadows Foundation Inc.

131 Adolph Gottlieb *Red and Blue No. 2* 1966. Oil on canvas, 152.4 × 121.9 (60 × 48). Courtesy the Marlborough Gallery, Inc, New York.

132 Robert Motherwell *Elegy to the Spanish Republic No. 34* 1953–54. Oil on canvas, 203.2 × 254 (80 × 100). Albright-Knox Art Gallery, Buffalo, New York. Gift of Seymour H. Knox, 1957.

133 Willem de Kooning *Door to the River* 1960. Oil on canvas, 203.2 × 177.8 (80 × 70). Collection of Whitney Museum of American Art, New York. Purchase, with funds from the Friends of the Whitney Museum of American Art, 60.63.

134 Franz Kline *Mahoning* 1956. Oil on canvas 203.2 × 254 (80 × 100). Collection of Whitney Museum of American Art, New York. Purchase, with funds from the Friends of the Whitney Museum of American Art, 57.10.

135 William Baziotes *The Pond* 1955. Oil on canvas, 182.9 × 167.6 (72 × 66). © The Detroit Institute of Arts, Founders Society Purchase, Friends of Modern Art Fund.

136 Hans Hofmann *Memoria in Aeternum* 1962. Oil on canvas, 213.3 × 183.2 (84 × 72$\frac{1}{8}$). Collection, The Museum of Modern Art, New York. Gift of the Artist.

137 Jackson Pollock *Number 14, 1951*. Oil on canvas, 146.5 × 269.5 (57$\frac{5}{8}$ × 106$\frac{1}{8}$). Tate Gallery, London.

138 Lee Krasner *Diptych* 1977–78. Collage on canvas, 167.6 × 289.6 (66 × 114). Courtesy Robert Miller Gallery, New York.

139 Aaron Siskind *Chicago 224, 1953*. Photograph. Courtesy Aaron Siskind.

140 Aaron Siskind *Pleasures and Terrors of Levitation 37, 1953*. Photograph. Courtesy Aaron Siskind.

141 Willem de Kooning *Untitled XII* 1982. Oil on canvas, 177.8 × 203.2 (70 × 80). Courtesy Xavier Fourcade, Inc, New York.

142 David Smith *Wagon I* 1963–64. Painted steel, 308.6 × 162.6 × 224.8 (121$\frac{1}{2}$ × 64 × 88$\frac{1}{2}$). National Gallery of Canada, Ottawa.

143 David Smith (left to right) *Cubi XVIII*, 1964. Stainless steel, 294 (115$\frac{3}{4}$). *Cubi XVII*, 1963. Stainless steel, 273.7 (107$\frac{3}{4}$). *Cubi XIX*, 1964. Stainless steel, 287.3 (113$\frac{1}{8}$). Marlborough-Gerson Gallery Inc, New York.

144 Barnett Newman *Broken Obelisk* 1963–67. Cor-ten steel. Photo courtesy Lippincott, Inc.

145 Barnett Newman *First Station* 1958. Magna on canvas, 198.1 × 152.4 (78 × 60). National Gallery of Art, Washington, D.C. Robert and Jane Meyerhoff Collection.

146 Clyfford Still *Oil on Canvas July 1974*. Oil on canvas, 289.6 × 436.9 (114 × 172). San Francisco Museum of Art, Collection of the Estate of Clyfford Still.

147 Mark Rothko *Four Darks in Red* 1958. Oil on canvas, 259.1 × 294.6 (102 × 116$\frac{1}{4}$). Collection of Whitney Museum of American Art, New York. Mr and Mrs Eugene M.

Schwartz, Mrs Samuel A. Seaver and Charles Simon, 68.9.

148 Mark Rothko, Houston Chapel, 1964–67. Photo Menil Foundation, Houston.

149 Mark Rothko *Untitled* 1969. Acrylic on canvas, 172.7 × 152.4 (68 × 60). Private Collection, Oklahoma City.

150 Anselm Kiefer *Maikäfer flieg (Cockchafer, fly)* 1974. Oil on burlap, 220 × 300 (86⅝ × 118). Saatchi Collection, London.

151 Julian Schnabel *Humanity Asleep* 1982. Painted ceramic relief on wood, 275 × 365.8 (108¼ × 144). Courtesy Leo Castelli/Mary Boone.

152 Kenneth Noland *Via Blues* 1967. Acrylic on canvas, 228.9 × 670.6 (90⅛ × 264). Collection Robert A. Rowan. Courtesy André Emmerich Gallery, New York.

153 Ibram Lassaw *Monoceros* 1952. Iron and brass, 108 × 62.2 × 46.4 (42½ × 24½ × 18¼). The Metropolitan Museum of Art, New York. Promised Gift of Muriel Kallis Newman. The Muriel Kallis Steinberg Newman Collection.

154 Mark di Suvero *Hankchampion* 1960. Wood and chains, 196.2 × 378.5 × 266.7 (77¼ × 149 × 105). Collection of Whitney Museum of American Art, New York. Gift of Mr and Mrs Robert C. Scull, 73.85.

155 Jasper Johns *Field Painting* 1963–64. Oil on canvas with objects, 182.9 × 93.4 (72 × 36¾). Collection The Artist. © Richard Serra, Robert Rauschenberg, Jasper Johns, Courtesy Leo Castelli Gallery, New York.

156 Louis Kahn in the auditorium of Kimbell Art Museum, Fort Worth, Texas, 1969–72. Photo Robert Wharton, courtesy Kimbell Art Museum, Fort Worth.

157 Helen Frankenthaler *Mountains and Sea* 1952. Oil on canvas, 220 × 297.8 (86⅝ × 117¼). Collection the Artist, on loan to the National Gallery of Art, Washington, D.C.

158 Morris Louis *Point of Tranquility* 1959–60. Magna on canvas, 258.2 × 344.9 (101¾ × 135¾). Hirshhorn Museum and

Sculpture Garden, Smithsonian Institution, Washington, D.C. Gift of Joseph H. Hirshhorn, 1966.

159 Helen Frankenthaler *Blue Territory* 1955. Oil on canvas, 287 × 147.3 (113 × 58). Collection of Whitney Museum of American Art, New York.

160 Anthony Caro *Early One Morning* 1962. Acrylic and metal sculpture, 289.6 × 619.8 × 335.3 (114 × 244 × 132). Tate Gallery, London.

161 Barry Flanagan *Large Leaping Hare* 1982. Gilded bronze, 188 × 176.5 × 112.4 (74 × 69½ × 44¼). From the Patsy R. and Raymond D. Nasher Collection, Dallas, Texas.

162 Walter Tandy Murch *Gear* 1950. Oil on canvas, 58.5 × 41 (23 × 61). Thyssen-Bornemisza Collection, Lugano, Switzerland.

163 Philip Guston *Ancient Wall* 1976. Oil on linen, 203.2 × 237.5 (80 × 93½). Hirshhorn Museum and Sculpture Garden, Smithsonian Institution, Washington, D.C. Museum Purchase, 1987.

164 Robert Rauschenberg *Choke* 1964. Oil and silkscreen on canvas, 152.4 × 121.9 (60 × 48). Washington University Gallery of Art, St Louis.

165 Frank Stella *Arbeit Macht Frei* 1958. Black enamel on canvas, 215.9 × 310 (85 × 122). Collection of Mr and Mrs Graham Gund. Photo Greg Heins.

166 Dan Flavin *Untitled (Homage to Barnett Newman)* 1969. Fluorescent fixtures with red, yellow and blue fluorescent bulbs, 243.8 × 121.9 (96 × 48). © Dan Flavin, Courtesy Leo Castelli Gallery, New York.

167 Brice Marden *Annunciation* 1978, installation view. Pace Gallery, New York.

168 Richard Serra *Splashing* 1968. Lead, indeterminate dimensions. © Richard Serra, Robert Rauschenberg, Jasper Johns, Courtesy Leo Castelli Gallery, New York.

169 Ad Reinhardt *Abstract Painting No. 5* 1962. Oil on canvas, 152.4 × 152.4 (60 × 60). Tate Gallery, London.

Index